THE INUIT IMAGINATION

Arctic Myth and Sculpture

THE INUIT

HAROLD SEIDELMAN
& JAMES TURNER

IMAGINATION

DOUGLAS & McINTYRE
VANCOUVER/TORONTO

Douglas & McIntyre Ltd.
1615 Venables Street
Vancouver, British Columbia
V5L 2H1

Canadian Cataloguing in Publication Data

Seidelman, Harold.
    The Inuit Imagination

ISBN 1-55054-102-1

1. Inuit—Canada—Sculpture.* 2. Inuit—Canada—Religion
and mythology.* I.Turner, James E.   II.Title.

E99.E7S45 1993   730'.89'971071   C93-091632-8

Photography by Michael Neill
Design by Michael Solomon
Editing by Brian Scrivener
Set in Simoncini Garamond and Imago by PrimeType, Toronto
Printed and bound in Canada by D.W. Friesen and Sons Ltd.

CONTENTS

COMMENTS BY DAVID RUBEN PIQTOUKUN

Growing up in the Arctic in the 1960s, I saw the final transition from the old way of life. For a young boy it was not easy to understand the reluctance of my father's generation to adopt a settled life. I could see their restlessness. They looked on hunting for caribou and seals as their real life, and hunting meant much more than a search for food.

For most of each year, I was away at church boarding schools where I received an education in forgetting. Our teachers were not able to understand or appreciate Inuit culture. We learned from them that our *tupilaks* (spirits) were evil. But I remember thinking that the Christian spirits were evil, too. When I returned to Paulatuk in the summer, my father would say that I knew how to count the caribou but I did not know how to hunt them.

During the years that I have earned my living as an artist, I have tried to come to terms with my culture. I have travelled extensively in the north, learning from other artists and sharing my own limited knowledge. At times, I have doubted that a coherent culture could be reassembled out of the few fragments that have survived in the chaos and confusion of the modern world. So much has been forgotten, and the Inuit have learned to see the world through the white man's perspective.

Reading *The Inuit Imagination* has given me new hope that the important values of the traditional life can be salvaged. My friends Harold Seidelman and James Turner have managed to integrate contemporary Inuit art with the stories, songs and customs of the old ways. I know that many of the artists whose work is represented here will be pleased that someone has attempted to understand their sculptures. They will be surprised that outsiders have been able to find so much meaning in Inuit art.

The authors have captured the seriousness of the traditions and also the humour of the Inuit, present even at times of hardship and sorrow. Their book reminds us of the importance of the imaginative life in every culture. I felt proud to remember the physical courage and the mental ingenuity with which my ancestors confronted their difficult life. Reading *The Inuit Imagination* and experiencing the sculptures, I felt again the powers of words and images, the powers of the spirits, to help us be ourselves.

Toronto   David Ruben Piqtoukun
December 1992

FOREWORD BY GEORGE SWINTON

The Inuit Imagination is an imaginative and daring book. In concept and execution it demands that southern readers abandon their accustomed ways of linear thinking and rely instead on their innate faculty of apprehending. Such understanding comes from sensing and being able to make connective leaps informed by, inevitably and alas, a degree of familiarity with traditions and mythology. I say "alas" because far too few of us have such knowledge. Yet without it many aspects of meaning are hidden, and the reader is uneasily confronted by subtle segments of myths and legends that stand for the whole.

The parts—images and ideas—come from the world of Inuit stories and oral traditions. They beckon us to share with the Inuit their understanding of the World or Existence, not through reason but through myths and legends, just as we in our childhood gained an understanding of our own world through fairy tales and stories we heard from our parents or grandparents, or in places of worship. I suppose modern youth receive their poetry and mythology through tapes and television....

In the Arctic, the belief in the spirit world lingers. In June 1990, while visiting in Baker Lake, I was called to visit Francis Kalloar, lying on his death bed. He suffered from what he called "a dog spirit in my stomach." Some time ago he had killed his dog, which, he said, "was no good." He got another one. But very soon he found out that the new dog wasn't any better. He then realized that he had killed the first dog unjustly and now the dog's spirit had returned to take revenge by settling in his stomach. Kalloar knew he was dying because he had offended the dog's spirit. The doctor and the nurses could not convince him otherwise. For Kalloar it was simply justice being done.

This book abounds in references to the Inuit spirit world and introduces us to many legends and sacred songs. In typical Inuit manner these have been strategically and effectively placed within a cumulative scheme of interrelated parts. The stories substantiate each other in content and method without the sentimentalities of their popularized versions, and without the kind of intellectualizations and rationalizations so customary in academic writing. They become synthesized rather than analyzed, all of which is highly reminiscent of one of Knud Rasmussen's most famous anecdotes.

> For several evenings we had discussed rules of life and taboo customs without getting beyond a long and circumstantial statement of all that was permitted and all that was forbidden. Everyone knew precisely what had to be done in any given situation, but whenever I put in my query: "Why?", they could give no answer. They regarded it, and very rightly, as unreasonable that I should require not only an account, but also a justification, of their religious principles. [The shaman] Aua had as usual been the spokesman, and as he was still unable to answer my questions, he rose to his feet, and as if seized by

a sudden impulse, invited me to go outside with him.... Ragged white clouds raced across the sky, and when a gust of wind came tearing over the ground, our eyes and mouths were filled with snow. Aua looked at me full in the face, and pointing out over the ice, where the snow was being lashed about in waves by the wind, he said:

"In order to hunt well and live happily, man must have calm weather. Why this constant succession of blizzards and all this needless hardship for men seeking food for themselves and those they care for? Why? Why?"

After they visited several families shivering in their cheerless igloos, Aua answered Rasmussen's question by saying finally, "[We] explain nothing, we believe nothing, but in what I have just shown you lies our answer to all you ask."

When I first went north in 1957 I was struck by that existential attitude of the Inuit. It fortunately happened to coincide with my own and I have therefore felt myself very much at home in the north. And so I feel myself in harmony with Seidelman's and Turner's methodology and the content of their book. They provide a thoughtful and rich introduction to Inuit imagination and also to Inuit lifestyle and world view manifested in their stories and myths.

Equally, their bringing together of a collection of contemporary Inuit sculptures, which represent the best of Inuit art, with the traditional myths, stories and songs points to the inexorable relationship between the two forms of expression and how they reinforce one another. While I have always contended that even the less good Inuit art gives some (mostly unconscious) evidence of Inuit self-affirmation, the best contains the spiritual values around which this book is formed. Those values emerge from the stone or bone or ivory, and on wall-hangings, prints and drawings, in strength and subtlety, in simple or complex forms, but always in harmony with Inuit tradition and existence, brought forth through Inuit sensibility and imagination.

George Swinton

PREFACE AND ACKNOWLEDGEMENTS

The Inuit world extends over a vast area across the Canadian north from Greenland to Alaska and beyond, reaching down as far as the southern limits of Hudson Bay. In time, it extends from the present back more than 2000 years into the past. Over these great expanses of space and time, there was a fundamental unity of Inuit culture due to the constraints of a harsh environment, a nomadic lifestyle based on a slowly changing hunting technology, and a common framework of beliefs. With very few resources, an ingenious people created a material and spiritual culture that evoked disbelief and admiration when it became known to the outside world.

The earliest recorded contacts of the modern period began with the first voyage of Martin Frobisher in 1576. There followed the fruitless search for a northwest passage, the fur trading of the Hudson's Bay Company, and extensive commercial whaling by Scottish and American whalers in the nineteenth century. These activities brought the Inuit of the coastal regions into progressively greater contact with Europeans. In the early years of this century, Anglican and Catholic missionary activity became widespread in the Canadian Arctic and began to displace the earlier Inuit beliefs. The first contacts with outsiders were sporadic and did not produce the profound changes seen in recent times. In fact, the early explorers, fur traders, whalers and missionaries had to adapt to Inuit ways or to depend on the local population in order to survive in the north. This has now changed almost completely. In the modern world of schools, airplanes, prefabricated housing, snowmobiles and satellite television, the remarkable adaptations evolved over countless centuries are no longer essential for physical survival. In this new environment, it is difficult at first to believe that anything can have survived from the traditional life.

The recent period of cultural upheaval has been accompanied by an outpouring of artistic activity that has gained worldwide recognition. This volume brings together a collection of contemporary Inuit sculptures produced in many areas of the Canadian north. The unifying theme of this collection is that the sculptures are all inspired by the stories, legends and myths and by the religious beliefs of the traditional culture. It is our aim to interpret these carvings in terms that are significant in the culture that created them. The production of sculptures, drawings, and prints in the last four decades seems to have responded to a deep need of a people undergoing a difficult transition to communicate their experiences and beliefs to the outside world. In the words of a Baker Lake artist, Ruby Angrnanaaq, "the prints and drawings are our way of sharing our thoughts of the past and present life with the southern people; they are the messages that we are sending out to the rest of the world."

Despite this desire to communicate, the themes and symbolism that are so obviously present in much of contemporary Inuit art have been difficult to interpret. In almost every region of the north, imaginative carvings are made of winged creatures, mermaids and grotesque animal forms. What are the meanings of the exaggerated eyes and outsized hands, the double images, the multiple faces, the ecstatic drum dancers, the half-human creatures, and the anthropomorphic shapes that appear so frequently? Too often these intriguing sculptures have been given uninformative descriptions, such as "animal composition," "transformations," "spirits" and "legendary creatures," with no further explanation. With a few exceptions, the creators of these mysterious objects have been reluctant to interpret their sculptures in any detail. One explanation of this reluctance is that outside influences, particularly Christian beliefs, have led to a devaluation of the traditions that inspire these sculptures. A second explanation is the difficulty of communicating concepts and motivations between very different cultures. A third significant factor is that asking questions is considered rude and immature in the traditional culture. There is an Inuit saying that the white men have two major faults — they are always washing and they are always asking questions.

Many admirers of Inuit art have been content to live with this uncertainty, enjoying instead the perfection of form and composition or a sentimental identification with a remote way of life. The approach that we adopt in these pages is very different in the belief that attempting to understand the sources of the Inuit imagination will deepen the appreciation of its expression in art. In our view, the narrative tradition interpreted in a wide sense is the key to unlocking this imaginative world. The ancient stories and the beliefs that they express continue to have a strong influence on Inuit life, an influence that has found a new expression in modern Inuit art.

It is a pleasure to acknowledge the many valuable contributions made by friends and colleagues who have shared with us their interest in Inuit art. Their suggestions, encouragement and constructive criticisms have been very helpful in the preparation of this work. In particular, we would like to express our appreciation to the following: Manasie Akpaliapik, Scott Amacker, Sandra Barz, Beverly and Irwin Bernick, Jean Blodgett, Marshall Campion, Cynthia Cook, John Cowan, Bernadette Driscoll, Dr. Norman Epstein, Dr. and Mrs. Stanley Epstein, David Ford, Henry Ford, Nelson Graburn, Norman Hallendy, James Houston, Patricia and Ted Leishman, Odette Leroux, Richard Martin, Lois and Daniel Miller, Marybelle Mitchell, David Ruben Piqtoukun, David Rapport, Gwen Rattle, Dr. Peeter Reichman, Marie Routledge, Esther and Samuel Sarick, Dr. Reuben Schucher, Hans-Gunther Schwarz, Sandy and Seymour Seligman, Charlotte and Lewis Steinberg, William Taylor, Darlene Wight, Craig Williamson, and Norman Zepp.

Our special thanks are due to Mary Craig, Terry Ryan and George Swinton for their always expert knowledge and advice, and to Michael Neill for his help with the photography. With love and appreciation, the many contributions of Rosalie, Carrie and Lani Seidelman are gratefully acknowledged. We are also grateful to the staffs of Canadian Arctic Producers, Eva Klassen and Lauren Venchiarutti; the Inuit Arts section of the Department of Indian and Northern Affairs, Ingo Hessel, Jeanne L'Esperance, and Maria Muehlen; La Fédération des Cooperatives du Nouveau Québec,

James McDonagh, Peter Murdoch, and Richard Murdoch; the North West Company, Inuit Art Marketing Service, Quintin Finlay, Denise Gagnon and Jeanne Pattison; and the West Baffin Eskimo Cooperative Ltd., Leslie Boyd, James Manning, Janet Mayhew, and John Westren. Tracy Fairchild assisted greatly in the preparation of the many drafts of the manuscript. The interest and professionalism of Scott McIntyre, Brian Scrivener, Michael Solomon and others at Douglas & McIntyre made the challenges of the editing and production process an enjoyable experience. Without their help, we may not have reached the shore. Finally, we would like to thank our families for their patience and understanding as the book developed.

When I was young, every day was a beginning of some new thing and every evening ended with the glow of the next day's dawn. Now I have only the old stories and songs to fall back on, the songs I sang myself in the days when I delighted to challenge my comrades to a song contest in the feasting house.

Ivaluardjuk, Igloolik
recorded in 1923
by Knud Rasmussen

1. Inuit Stories

STORYTELLING may have been the earliest art form. It is an essential means of individual and social expression common to all peoples. Every culture has evolved a framework of stories to describe and to reconcile the complementary worlds of reality and imagination. In cultures without writing, the storyteller has a particularly important role. Far more than simple entertainment, the stories represent the cultural memory and imaginative history of the community. They encode the values considered important for survival. Both the commonplace and the important events of life are understood in relation to these stories and the beliefs they express.

In the traditional world of the Inuit, every community preserved a collection of stories and songs that were considered its own. The stories fulfilled many purposes — to pass the time, to entertain, to record moments of joy and sorrow, to instruct and to preserve important values. Some stories were designed to shorten the long nights of winter by sending the listeners to sleep. The highest praise for one of these tales was to say that no one had ever heard the end of it. Inuit stories describe hunting accidents, abductions, personal conflicts, the cruel fates of orphans and old people, epic journeys, the origin of the natural world, and the spirit world. As in all folklore, there are numerous animal fables and stories dealing with healing and morality. Many stories were directed to children, teaching them by example instead of by punishments and scolding. The more important legends were repeated in relatively unchanged form over many generations. Others, which may have been told once or twice and then forgotten, were simple improvisations on events of passing interest, such as the loss of a seal while hunting or the beauty of summer.

Regrettably, the incursion of modern society has broken the chain of oral transmission of many traditional stories in the north. Most of our knowledge of the Inuit narrative tradition is due to the efforts of a small number of individuals who recorded stories when they were more current. William Parry and George Lyon led a British Navy expedition from 1821 to 1823, searching for the elusive Northwest Passage. They wintered in the Igloolik region on the northwest coast of Hudson Bay. Their accounts contain the first descriptions of the belief systems of the Inuit of the central regions. Lyon's curiosity about Inuit customs even extended to allowing himself to be tattooed on his arms in the style of Inuit women.

In the effort to document and understand traditional Inuit life, there are two names that deserve special mention, Franz Boas and Knud Rasmussen. Boas spent one eventful year in 1883-84 among a group of German scientists participating in an International Polar Year, a year of cooperative arctic research. Their base camp was located near present-day Pangnirtung on Baffin Island. Trained as a geographer, Boas travelled extensively and gathered an astonishing amount of information about Inuit culture in a relatively short time. During his year in the Arctic, he observed at first hand the importance of storytelling in Inuit social life.

> A favourite amusement during the long winter nights is telling tales and composing songs. Old traditions are always related in a highly ceremonious manner. The narrator takes off his outer jacket, pulls the hood over his head, and sits down in the rear part of the hut, turning his face toward the wall, and then tells his story slowly and solemnly. All the stories are related in a very abridged form, the substance being supposed to be known. The form is always the same, and should the narrator happen to say one word otherwise than is customary he will be corrected by the listeners. Children tell one another fables and sing short songs. Comic songs making fun of any person are great favourites.

Almost forty years later, Knud Rasmussen organized and led the now legendary Fifth Thule Expedition, also known as the Danish Ethnographical Expedition to Arctic North America, 1921-24. Rasmussen had planned this expedition as early as 1902 when he first studied the customs and mythology of the Greenland Inuit. The many publications that resulted form the core of our knowledge of traditional Inuit culture. Thule was the name from ancient mythology given by Rasmussen to the remote outpost that he established with Peter Freuchen in 1910 in the lands of the Polar Eskimo on the northwest coast of Greenland. Over the next twenty-one years, it served as their base for seven expeditions.

Rasmussen, Freuchen, the anthropologist Kaj Birket-Smith and the archaeologist Therkel Matthiassen established headquarters for two years on Danish Island in northern Hudson Bay, from which they thoroughly documented all aspects of the culture of the surrounding areas. In March 1923, Rasmussen set out with two Greenland Inuit companions, Miteq and Anarulunguaq, on a sledge journey to the Pacific Ocean that would last one and a half years. All the equipment they took with them was carried on two twenty-foot-long sledges pulled by twenty-four dogs. During this epic trip, Rasmussen discovered the fundamental unity of the Inuit world, both material and spiritual. Fluent in Greenlandic, he was able to make himself understood in every area. Throughout his journey, he heard tales very similar to the stories and legends that he had heard as a child in Greenland; "when I began telling of the Greenland folk tales to the company here, it turned out that they knew them already; and were, moreover, themselves astonished to find that a stranger should be acquainted with what they regarded as their own particular legends."

Many others have added essential elements to our knowledge of Inuit stories and their significance. The Anglican missionary Archibald Fleming devoted his life to the scattered people of the Canadian Arctic. Beginning his career in the north in 1910, he was unusually sensitive to the importance of the many stories that he heard in his travels. Despite his sympathetic attitudes, he described his difficulties with the problem of understanding Inuit thought processes. "That they accepted their mystical stories as true and that these had far reaching implications influencing their life and conduct could not be doubted. But behind their myths there appeared to be a sincere attempt to interpret the problems of

1. Henry Napartuk   Kuujjuaraapik 1978   *Transformation*
The piercing eye is a reminder that the shaman is the one who sees with an inner vision.

existence." In our own more skeptical time, we might make the same comment about Fleming's Christian stories and beliefs.

More recently, Raymond de Coccola has written a very unromanticized account of his twelve years from 1937 to 1949 as a Catholic missionary in the central arctic. With great insight he describes the struggle for survival of the Barren Land Eskimo, an isolated, impoverished group of people. His account emphasizes the important role of stories, legends and myths in their everyday life. At unexpected moments, songs and stories were used by all to express emotions and ideas. Father de Coccola was present when, without any warning, a small child asked, "Grandmother, tell me about Tarakapfaluk, the spirit who lives at the bottom of the sea." The grandmother then stopped what she was doing and told a simple account of the ancient legend. Her story began in a way common to all folklores. "Her name was Tara. She was a little girl who didn't like men. But one day a bird of the sea came and took the form of a handsome man. And she fell in love with him. . . ."

The Inuit tell many stories in the form of anecdotes, short remembrances of ordinary or unusual occurrences.

> "Men and the beasts are much alike," said Aua [to Rasmussen] sagely. "And so it was our fathers believed that men could be animals for a time, then men again." So he told the story of a bear he had once observed, hunting walrus like a human being, creeping up and taking cover, till it got within range, when it flung a huge block of ice that struck its victim senseless.

Aua seems to be recounting a personal experience, but Rasmussen was probably aware that this story had been told for generations in the arctic. One hundred years before in the same region, George Lyon recorded a similar story from an Igloolik hunter's account. Whether polar bears can hunt in this way is conjecture, but the significant part of the story is its beginning, "Men and the beasts are much alike." Peter Freuchen also observed the narrative abilities of the same storyteller; "In the evening Aua built our snowhouses and stories concerning all the points of interest we passed poured from his lips. Here a number of persons had starved to death; at this lake great battles had taken place; at another point a large stone had killed a man while Aua looked on—the blood was still on it and would never disappear because the man had been innocent."

From the perspectives of a literate culture, it is easy to underestimate the strength of the oral tradition. The most elaborate legends may have an historical basis. During the Fifth Thule Expedition, Rasmussen attempted to learn of any recollections of the ill-fated Franklin expedition. The veteran arctic explorer Sir John Franklin had left England in 1845 with 129 officers and men on two ships to search for a Northwest Passage. After more than seventy-five years had passed, Rasmussen was successful in gathering information about the disaster from several informants. He also learned that the Inuit around Pelly Bay had many reminiscences of the John Ross expedition that had wintered in that region in 1829. The supplies left behind by these strangers—wood, iron, nails, chains and iron hoops—were still being used a century later in the form of knives, arrow heads, harpoon heads, salmon spears, caribou spears and hooks. Raymond de Coccola interviewed a hunter whose family had detailed recollections of the fate of the Franklin crew. More surprising, Archibald Fleming learned of a place called White Man's Island where the Inuit believed that white men had lived many years ago. He concluded that Martin Frobisher and his ships had wintered at that location in 1578, considerably more than three hundred years before.

One story collected by Rasmussen near Bathurst Inlet is more clearly a product of the imagination, yet it does make an obvious point. The young storyteller Netsit told of two hunters, one of whom has killed a caribou and the other a wolf. They have an argument about which animal has more hairs. To settle the argument, they decide to pull out the hairs one by one. This takes so long that both hunters die of starvation. The story uses humour to warn against pride and any kind of obsessive behaviour. Do not waste time on arguments, especially useless ones. The storyteller concluded with the sensible observation, "That is what happens when people busy themselves with aimless things and insignificant trifles." Another story that warns against pride and lack of attention to the important things is the tale of the owl and the marmot told to Rasmussen by Kivkarjuk, a Caribou Eskimo.

> There was once an owl who went out hunting, and seeing a marmot outside its house, it flew towards it and, sitting down in front of the entrance, sang: "I have barred the way of a land beast to its home. Come and fetch it and bring two sledges."
>
> But the marmot answered: "O mighty owl, spread your legs a little wider apart, and show me that powerful chest." And the owl hearing this was proud of its broad chest, and spread its legs wider apart.

**2. David Ruben Piqtoukun
Paulatuk, Toronto 1992 *Owl and Weasel***
A version of the famous story where the pride
of the owl is confronted by the cunning of the
weasel.

Then the marmot cried: "Wider, wider still." And the owl feeling even prouder
than before spread its legs a little wider still, and stretched its chest as far as it
could. But then the marmot slipped between its legs and ran off into its hole.

Raymond de Coccola heard the same story of the owl and the ground squirrel,
an account that differs only in one detail added to the ending. Pleased with the
squirrel's compliments, the owl spread his legs as far as possible and inhaled
more air to swell his chest. "'That's beautiful!' exclaimed the squirrel as he
darted between the owl's legs, biting the latter's crotch before disappearing into
his underground home."

Rasmussen recorded many more animal fables in his travels. One is the story
of the raven and the loon told among the Caribou Eskimo.

In the olden days, all birds were white. And then one day the raven and the loon
fell to drawing patterns on each other's feathers. The raven began and when it had
finished the loon was so displeased with the pattern that it spat all over the raven
and made it black all over. And since that day all ravens have been black. But the
raven was so angry that it fell upon the loon and beat it so about the legs that it
could hardly walk. And that is why the loon is such an awkward creature on land.

Franz Boas related the very similar Central Eskimo story of the owl and the
raven.

The owl and the raven were fast friends. One day the raven made a new dress,
dappled with white and black, for the owl who in return made a pair of boots of

whalebone for the raven and then began to make a white dress. But when he was about to try it on, the raven kept hopping about and would not sit still. The owl got angry and said: "Now sit still or I shall pour out the lamp over you." As the raven continued hopping about, the owl fell into a passion and poured the oil upon it. Then the raven cried "Qaq! Qaq!" and since that day has been black all over.

Beyond the simple humour of these stories, they are clearly intended to teach children to be sensible and patient, to avoid anger and to keep their friends. In addition, they have a very practical purpose. By means of vivid images, they bring to life and make unforgettable important aspects of the behaviour of the animals on which Inuit life depended. At a deeper level, the stories say that in a former time animals and people were very much alike. The raven, the loon and the owl are all experimenting with their identities, only to learn that their ordinary existences are preferable.

Another witness to the importance of stories in traditional life was Diamond Jenness, who served as an anthropologist with the Canadian Arctic Expedition in 1913-18. He was frequently surprised by the spontaneity of song and story creation; "the day after we reached their settlement the Coppermine River Eskimos had a song about us, which was simply a new set of words adapted to

3. Mathew Aqigaaq   Baker Lake 1974   *Double Vision*
Balanced between two worlds, the angakoq looks to the future and the past. He sees the worlds of reality and imagination with an outer and an inner vision.

an old tune. Ikpakhuak was so amused over an adventure of mine with a wolf that before I had finished my story he had improvised a song about it; whenever he was at a loss for any word he simply filled up the gap with the meaningless syllables of *ai ye yanga*." In his first months in the arctic, Jenness travelled for a time with a small group returning from Coronation Gulf to homes on Victoria Island after an absence of two or three years. He was greatly touched by their joy in recognizing each prominent lake and hill and by the memories of earlier days that these landmarks called up.

Gontran de Poncins was a visitor from France to the region of Gjoa Haven and Pelly Bay in the late 1930s. Arriving unexpectedly in one igloo, he had not been there more than five minutes when he heard laughter coming from an adjoining igloo. "Bending forward, I looked in and saw — my own image. They were mimicking me . . . and the mimicry was done with so much art, with such perfection in reproduction of the intonation of my voice that I was stupefied." When he travelled with an Inuit family, de Poncins soon realized his comparative limitations in observing the world about him. "Where I saw space devoid of life, my Eskimos saw life. Again and again, Utak and his wife would stop, bend forward, stare at the ground, or leave the trail and go to the right and left, then come back smiling. . . . Nothing escapes them and their observation is incessant. For a stone that is not in its normal position they will stop, murmur, discuss; and then on they go with me behind."

The highly developed visual imagination that de Poncins observed enabled the Inuit to take possession of a landscape that seemed featureless to visitors. When about to cross for the first time from Igloolik to Pond Inlet on Baffin Island, Peter Freuchen was given a detailed description of the route that his small group should follow. "I carefully wrote down all the names they mentioned while my Eskimos just remembered them. The good thing about Eskimo names is that they always make places easily recognizable. Thus we had to go to Pingo, which means a round mountain top; then to Kuksuaq, meaning the great river; then to Tassersuaq, meaning the large lake; and so on across Baffin Island." In 1957, the Dutch ethnologist Geert van den Steenhoven studied the *ilageet* relationships among the Inuit of the Pelly Bay region. When he asked Tungilik to describe these complex food-sharing partnerships, he received a memorable reply: "Somewhere everyone is related to everyone here. But if you wish to know who right now really want to belong together, then take a look at how our tents are grouped or, in winter, how precisely our igloos are grouped. You will learn much from that." Tungilik found it easier to give an immediate visual explanation for a set of relationships that would be very difficult to detail in words.

From 1958 to 1966, Duncan Pryde managed some of the most remote trading posts of the Hudson's Bay Company, first at Spence Bay and then at Perry Island and Bathurst Inlet. He shared with the Inuit in these regions an almost traditional life. Returning one time from hunting seals on the ice, he found how comfortable a snowhouse could be. "It was warm and cozy; we brought out our tobacco and rolled a cigarette or pulled out a pipe. . . . The evenings were spent in storytelling and reenactments of the day's kill. Sometimes if a hunter had sat out on the ice all day long without getting a seal, he composed a song, singing that night the words he thought of while waiting for the seals that didn't come."

4. Levi Alasua Pirti Smith   Akulivik-Povungnituk 1968   *Transformation*
"Many animals have changed to human beings before the very eyes of the hunters, and changed as quickly back again. They can be offended by scornful words, and the hunter who mocks the caribou, for example, or the seal, will suddenly find himself stricken down by sickness or afflicted with constant ill luck" (Jenness, 180).

Pryde described one old blind woman at Perry Island as the mental archive of the community. "Not only did she remember all that happened to members of the band there, but she was the repository for all the fantastic stories and legends that the people treasured. An essential part of every drum dance was the break in dancing in which Arnayuk would tell a legend or tale."

In the Inuit world, the ability to tell stories well was a highly respected accomplishment. A skilled storyteller was always a welcome guest in other communities. Storytelling was a performance art demanding both training and talent. Many stories were recited rhythmically with voice changes, chorus or drum accompaniment, exaggerated physical gestures, animal mimicry, hypnotic repetition and other very dramatic effects. It is important to remember that the stories were created in an oral tradition. When written down and translated for our benefit, they exist in a new form without their essential dramatic, musical and visual components. Some of the early collectors of stories reported that the dramatic skill of the storytellers was so great that a spectator could follow the stories quite easily even if he understood only a few words of the language. To judge by the evidence of a collection of stories of the Mackenzie Inuit gathered by Herbert Schwarz in the 1960s, these skills have survived into recent times.

> As I sat there and listened to his story there were times that I did not need to understand Eskimo to comprehend his tale. Felix Nuyaviak was not just a storyteller, but also a superb actor who lived and acted out the various parts in his story.
>
> With expressive motion he paddled his kayak, he threw a spear, he freed his lines, and he sang magic songs. Finally there was triumph and enjoyment on his face as with a great effort, he hauled the whale ashore and sprayed it with water as the ancient custom demanded. . . . For the first time in the Arctic I listened to the stories as they had been told in the past with all the drama, mimicry, humour and playacting of the storyteller who kept his audience spellbound with the magic of it all.

Separated from this performance aspect, many of the recorded stories are inevitably disappointing as literature. The written stories often begin or end abruptly or omit essential details. This is understandable since in most cases the listeners for whom the stories were intended knew them as well as their narrators did.

The following story describing the origin of seagulls was told by Davidialuk Alasua Amittu, an artist of the modern period who lived in the Povungnituk area of northern Quebec. Before his death in 1976, Davidialuk recorded numerous stories in his many prints, drawings and sculptures, leaving a unique documentary record of the narrative tradition. In the collection *Eskimo Stories*, he introduced another tale with these words; "The stories of the old people are like dreams; we do not know them too well. The old men used to tell the stories. We heard them this way . . ."

> They had set out on their summer migration, the women walking along the shore and the men in kayaks. The women got lost. They picked berries — all they could find to eat — and called out to their husbands that they were lost. It got dark and still they kept calling. One old woman kept calling "Where are you?" until she

turned into a seagull. All night long they walked with only the ripening red berries to eat. Then all the women and even the little children turned into seagulls and flew over the kayaks. There were no seagulls before this time. Sometimes they can see the seals in the water as they fly. The story goes that sometimes seagulls can eat people but actually people turned into seagulls.

This deceptively simple story contains many important features. A normal event in life conceals hidden dangers that lead to the most terrifying accident, the separation of the community. There is an intense struggle to survive, leading to a supernatural metamorphosis and the origin of seagulls. Children hearing this story would learn about the everpresent dangers of life, the closeness of the human and animal worlds, and how to recognize the cry of the seagull. The continuity of the storytelling tradition is shown by a very similar story recorded by the ethnologist Lucien M. Turner in the Ungava district of arctic Quebec almost one hundred years before.

> Some people in a boat desired to go around a point of land which projected far into the water. As the water there was always in a violent commotion under the end of the point which terminated in a high cliff, some of the women were requested to walk over the neck of land. One of them got out with her children in order to lighten the boat. She was directed to go over the place, and they promised to wait for her on the other side. The people in the boat had gone so far that their voices, giving the direction, became indistinct. The poor woman became confused and suspected they wanted to desert her. She remained about the cliff, constantly crying the last words she heard. She ultimately turned into a gull, and now shouts only the sound like "go over, goover, over, ove."

The details of the two stories are different but the major elements are the same. In both versions, a few words are sufficient to create some memorable dreamlike images. Both stories have an emotional appeal and much is left to the imagination. They centre on themes of separation and abandonment that occur very frequently in Inuit folklore. In the narrative tradition, there is no real distinction between historical accounts, legends and myths. As with these two stories, many others seem to have evolved from commonplace events. The simplest narratives are often related to the beliefs encoded in a complex mythology.

Lucien Turner collected numerous stories accounting for the origin of the different animals in addition to the legend of the seagull. These appealing narratives told generations ago among the Hudson Bay and Labrador Eskimo enshrine some important folk wisdom.

ORIGIN OF THE RAVEN

The raven was a man, who, while other people were collecting their household property preparatory to removing to another locality, called to them that they had forgotten to bring the lower blanket of deerskin used for a bed. This skin in the Eskimo language is called *kak*. The man used the word so often that they told him to get it himself. He hurried so much that he was changed into a raven, and now uses that sound for his note. Even to this day when the camp is being removed the raven flies over and shouts "Kak! Kak!" or, in other words, "Do not forget the blanket."

ORIGIN OF THE HARE

The hare was a child who was so ill treated and abused by the other people, because it had long ears, that it went to dwell by itself. When it sees anyone the ears are laid down on the back, for, if it hears the shout of a person, it thinks they are talking of its long ears. It has no tail, because it did not formerly have one.

ORIGIN OF THE WOLF

The wolf was a poor woman, who had so many children that she could not find enough for them to eat. They became so gaunt and hungry that they were changed into wolves, constantly roaming over the land seeking food. The cry of the mother may be heard as she strives to console her hungry children, saying that food in plenty will soon be found.

ORIGIN OF THE HAWK

Among the people of a village was a woman who was noted for the shortness of her neck. She was so constantly teased and tormented about it that she often sat

5. Peter Assapa　Povungnituk 1982 *Insect*
Charlie Ugyuk　Spence Bay 1989 *Insect*
There was an exaggerated fear of worms and insects, especially bees. Flies were carried as amulets to make a person invulnerable since flies were difficult to catch. Each spring, they seemed to return from the land of the dead.

for hours on the edge of high places. She changed into a hawk, and now when she sees anyone she immediately exclaims, "Kea! Kea! Kea! who, who, who was it that cried 'short neck?'"

ORIGIN OF LICE

Lice are supposed to drop from the body of a huge spirit, dwelling in the regions above, who was punished by having these pests constantly torment him. In his rage to free himself the lice dropped down upon the people who condemned him to this punishment.

ORIGIN OF MOSQUITOES

A man had a wife who was negligent and failed to scrape his skin clothing properly when he returned from his expeditions. He endeavoured to persuade her to mend her ways and do as a wife should do. She was again directed to remove the accumulated layer of dirt from the man's coat. She petulantly took the garment and cleaned it in such a slovenly way that when the husband discovered the condition

6. Aisa Aviliaju Itukalla   Povungnituk 1992 *Insect*
Judas Ullulaq   Gjoa Haven 1990 *Insect*
Noah Annanack   Kangiqsualujjuaq 1980 *Insect Spirit*
Davidialuk Alasua Amittu   Povungnituk c. 1968 *Bee*
Flies were masters of the air with moods as unpredictable as the Great Spirit of the Air. The ever present louse appears in many stories. To appease Sedna, the shamans would remove the lice from her flowing hair.

7. Eli Sallualu Qinuajua   Povungnituk c. 1980   *Metamorphosis*
One of the most original and creative artists of arctic Quebec, Sallualu's complex anthropomorphic forms drawn from insects suggest the mysterious connections made in dreams and by the imagination.

of the coat he took some of the dirt from it and flung it after her. The particles changed into mosquitoes, and now (in spring) when the warm days come and the women have the labour of cleaning clothes to perform, the insects gather around them, and the women are thus reminded of the slovenly wife and what befell her.

ORIGIN OF THE SWALLOW

Some small children, who were extraordinarily wise, were playing at building toy houses on the edge of a high cliff near the village in which they dwelt. They were envied for their wisdom, and to them was given the name "Zulugagnak" or "like a raven," which was supposed to know all the past and future. While these children were thus amusing themselves, they were changed into small birds, which did not forget their last occupation, and even to this day they come to the cliffs, near the camps of the people, and build houses of mud, which they affix to the side of the rock. Even the raven does not molest them, and the Eskimo children love to watch the swallow build his *iglugiak* of mud.

ORIGIN OF THE GUILLEMOTS

While some children were playing on the level top of a high cliff overhanging the sea, the older children watched the younger ones lest they should fall down the bluff. Below them the sea was covered with ice, and the strip along the shore had not yet loosened to permit the seals to approach. Soon afterward a wide crack opened and the water was filled with seals, but the children did not observe them. The wind was cold, and the children romped in high glee, encouraging each other to greater exertion in their sports and shouted at the top of their voices. The men saw the seals and hastened to the shore to put their kayaks into the water to pursue them. At this the children increased their shouts, which frightened the seals till they dived out of sight. One of the men was angry, and exclaimed to the others, "I wish the cliff would topple over and bury those noisy children for scaring the seals." In a moment the cliff tipped over and the poor children fell among the fragments of huge rocks and stones at the bottom. Here they were changed into guillemots or sea-pigeons, with red feet, and even to this day they thus dwell among the debris at the foot of the cliffs next to the water of the sea.

ORIGIN OF THE SEA MAMMALS

A woman who had lost her husband lived among strangers. As they desired to change the place of their habitation, they resolved to journey to another point of land at a distance. The woman who was depending on charity had become a burden of which they wished to rid themselves. So they put all their belongings into the *umiak* (sealskin boat) and when they were on the way they seized the woman and cast her overboard. She struggled to regain the side of the boat, and when she seized it, the others cut off her fingers, which fell into the water and changed to seals, walrus, whales and white bears. The woman, in her despair, screamed her determination to have revenge for the cruelty perpetrated upon her. The thumb became a walrus, the first finger a seal, and the middle finger a white bear. When the former two animals see a man they try to escape lest they be served as the woman was. The white bear lives both on the land and in the sea, but when he perceives a man revengeful feelings fill him, and he determines to destroy the person who he thinks mutilated the woman from whose finger he sprang.

To our way of thinking, Inuit stories often seem fragmentary and capable of considerable expansion. The legend of the origin of the hare does not say that

8. Natar Ungalaq   Igloolik 1985   *Dying Father*
Not so long ago, sons and daughters had one last duty to
perform for their aging parents. Out of cruel necessity, a dying
father would command his favourite son to help him to die.
Natar Ungalaq shows an old man who has left his possessions
behind as his son leads him away from the living.

the child was ill treated almost certainly because it was an orphan. Otherwise it would have been protected. A common form of abuse (at least in stories) was to pull on the child's ears until they grew in length. Other versions of the legend of the origin of the sea mammals expand the rudimentary account recorded by Lucien Turner into the primary creation myth of their belief system. Why did the strangers in this legend desire to change their place of habitation? This is explained very frankly by the description Turner gives elsewhere of the relevant customs, an explanation that would not be needed by Inuit listeners.

> Aged people who have no relatives on whom they may depend for subsistence are often quietly put to death. When an old woman, for instance, becomes a burden to the community it is usual for her to be neglected until so weak from want of food that she will be unable to keep up with the people, who suddenly are seized with a desire to remove to a distant locality. If she regains their camp, well for her; otherwise, she struggles along until exhausted and soon perishes.

Despite the incompleteness and occasional incoherence of these origin stories, something of their force and significance survives translation. Herbert Schwarz collected many stories from one storyteller but, as he writes, "Some of these were just isolated fragments which I had to piece together." Even less fragmentary longer stories often have a tenuous logical coherence and outsiders may look in vain for some unambiguous meaning. There is rarely a sustained development of a central theme with clear moral conclusions. This is illustrated very well by the brief story of the creation of the caribou collected by Rasmussen, an account that raises many more questions than it answers.

> Once upon a time there were no caribou on the earth. But then there was a man who wished for caribou, and he cut a great hole deep in the ground, and up through this hole came caribou, many caribou. The caribou came pouring out, till the earth was almost covered with them. And when the man thought there were caribou enough for mankind, he closed up the hole again. Thus the caribou came up on earth.

Perhaps the prize for compression of details goes to the legend of the origin of the Inuit, recorded by Lucien Turner.

> A man was created from nothing. It was summer and he journeyed until he found a woman in another land. The two became man and wife, and from them sprang all the people dwelling there.

Turner evidently failed in his attempt to have a fuller explanation of this fable. These creation stories have a definite, pragmatic quality that does not invite the storyteller or the listener to interpret or to speculate. He writes, "It is extremely difficult to get the native to go beyond the immediate vicinity in which he lives while relating these stories and legends. They invariably maintain that it was 'here' that the event took place." It is notable that these stories do not involve gods or god-like beings but instead deal with ordinary men, women and children. Some interruption in normal behaviour leads to supernatural events and consequences, usually disastrous, follow.

When reading these stories, they seem at first to be little more than a sequence of strong visual images held together with a minimum use of repetitive language. Turner describes the old women relating the history of the former days often "interspersed with recitations apparently foreign to the thread of the legend." In their original cultural context, the dramatic emotional effects were often more important than the logical connections between the different parts of the stories. De Coccola noted that, in their stories, the Inuit simply accept the universe around them instead of trying to analyze it. "They are basically unemotional fatalists inclined to reduce their philosophy to a single expression: *Ayornartok* (it can't be helped)." This one word was used to dismiss all misfortunes; "There isn't anything one can do about it—that's destiny, that's life." A common saying was, "Today we are happy; tomorrow is a long way away."

In the late 1940s and early 1950s, the anthropologist Edmund Carpenter studied the Aivilik Eskimo living in the northwest coastal regions of Hudson Bay. He came to the conclusion that chronological sequence was of very little

9. Jonah Janesah Iqaluit 1980 *Angakoq's Dream*
The angakoq's familiar spirits help him on his spirit journey. The walrus-tusked shaman
faces backward so that he may regain the human world.

importance in their mythology. He described his difficulties in comprehending
one storyteller. "He was apparently uninterested in narrating his story from the
ground upward, for he began with the crisis, so to speak, and worked backward
and forward, with many omissions and repetitions, on the tacit assumption that
my mind worked in the same groove as his and that explanations were needless.
It produced the most extraordinary effect, one reminiscent of that achieved by
Joyce and other sophisticated writers who deliberately reject sequential time. I
was later forced to rearrange clusters of statements so that they represented an
historical sequence — only then did they become coherent to me."

Several decades before Carpenter's observations, Diamond Jenness had
made a similar complaint about the inability of the Copper Eskimo storytellers to
follow a logical train of thought; "a native will never tell a story straightforwardly
from beginning to end. He starts in the middle, returns on himself to explain
some allusion, and wanders backwards and forwards in this manner until he has
completed all he has to tell. He is easily diverted into another channel or another
subject. Direct questions, unless they are simple requests for an enlargement on
some remark he has just made, almost invariably confuse him, and he becomes
incoherent or silent. This explains to some extent the amazing variations in the
accounts that different natives give of the same event or story where the words
are not stereotyped into fixed formulae." Using almost the same terms as
Jenness, Gontran de Poncins also experienced difficulties in understanding an
Inuit storyteller. "He began in the middle, pronouncing directly the most important word in his mind. Then he went back to the beginning of a phrase and
started afresh. . . . Suddenly images would flow through his mind, but so many
that he could not reduce this chaos to order." De Poncins recognized that the

10. Osuitok Ipeelee   Cape Dorset c. 1975
Fox Wife
Osuitok explained that a woman could turn
into a fox. There is an old story that tells of
a hunter who came back from hunting to
find that his wife was missing. There was a
peculiar smell in the igloo and outside he
could see only fox tracks.

white man's way of putting his questions was usually counterproductive. "I would ask a question directly to begin with. Then I would have to attenuate it, explain in roundabout fashion what I was getting at."

In his influential book *Sculpture of the Eskimo*, George Swinton addresses the question of the lack of organization of Inuit narratives. He detects some positive qualities where others have found confusion. "The many versions, the disorganized and repetitious accounts are not at all surprising. Neither are the ambiguities, nor poor or fragmentary presentations. These hazards would not be encountered only by an Eskimo ethnologist; to me, they are part of the entire Eskimo system of life and aesthetics. The strength and vitality of Eskimo art, and one might also speak here of philosophy and thinking (both as a process and product), lie in an undifferentiated, syncretistic approach in which details can be repeated, omitted or even added without affecting the whole meaning. In this regard Eskimo art and thoughts are very much like television programs or serials with interruptions from commercials, distorted reception and added living-room conversations, but which — interruptions and conversations notwithstanding — can be readily understood almost in spite of themselves. It is this very casualness of communication, combined with the capacity to draw attention sufficient for understanding without learned commentaries, that is typical of Eskimo art and traditions."

An illustration can allow the viewer to participate in the telling of a story, selecting some elements for emphasis and rearranging the chronological sequence. This necessary visual element found expression in surprising ways among the Inuit. Archibald Fleming recorded his fascination with the complex string figures created from a light leather thong about six feet in length. "They illustrate the stories they tell by means of these representations and once you understand the art you have no difficulty in seeing the hunter stalking the caribou or the seal popping into its hole or the boat in the water or the bird hopping over the land." Another Anglican missionary, Donald Marsh, described some of these string figures as masterpieces of ingenuity and complexity. He observed the game played by two people who would pass the string back and forth, making progressively more complicated patterns until one of them could not think of another move. Marsh commented that this game rivalled chess for its logic and intricacy. Raymond de Coccola was also intrigued by the creative patterns formed in the string game, calling them "a concrete means of transmitting their inner thoughts." He learned to recognize a trotting caribou, a seal basking in the sun, an arctic hare running away from a fox, a man and woman embracing, male and female genitals, and many other figures. He believed that these almost unlimited patterns compensated for the absence of illustrated books or graphic art. Considering the origins of Inuit stories, it can be argued that their essential cores are conveyed much better by a visual medium than by any purely literary form.

2. The Spirit World

THE YOUNG HUNTER Netsit once told Rasmussen not to ask for the meaning of a particular story. "It is not always that we want a point in our stories if only they are amusing. It is only the white men that want a reason and an explanation of everything, and so our old men say that we should treat white men as children who always want their own way. If not they become angry and scold." To make his point, Netsit then went on to say, "Before we go to sleep I shall tell you another story that has still less meaning in it, but one that we think is good enough." Another time, a Polar Eskimo storyteller told Rasmussen that, even if they did not understand their stories, they believed them all the same. "Who can prove that what he does not understand is wrong? And is it not wiser to bow to it and obey, when you are too ignorant to draw up anything better yourself?"

Inuit narratives are rich in meaning but in ways that are difficult for us to recognize, since they are a reflection of a very different view of the world. Instead of an objective framework of cause and effect, the stories are set in a supernatural background that at first seems incomprehensible. For the storyteller this background was assumed and needed no explanation. Kaj Birket-Smith reported the reasoning given by a Polar Eskimo to account for the failure of a polar bear hunt. "There were no bears, because there is no ice, and there is no ice, because there is too much wind, and there is too much wind, because we have offended the powers." On this subject, Diamond Jenness described the Inuit as "a people who have no conception of our 'natural laws', but in their place have substituted a theory of spiritual causation in which there is no boundary between the possible and the impossible." In the Igloolik area, Orulo impatiently told Rasmussen that too much thought only leads to trouble. "We Eskimos do not concern ourselves with solving all riddles. We repeat the old stories in the way they were told to us and with the words we ourselves remember. . . . You always want these supernatural things to make sense, but we do not bother about that. We are content not to understand."

Josie Papialook is a contemporary Povungnituk artist well known for his cheerful prints of birds in full song, which he represents by colourful squiggling lines drawn across the prints. He is also well known for his sense of humour and his carefree attitude to life. Like many other Inuit artists, he has often wondered aloud why the white people are so interested in his drawings. Papialook does not ask that his art be understood by others, and in fact he claims that his artwork is a joke. In the 1976 Povungnituk print catalogue, he is quoted as saying that his real art lies in writing his name on the snow. "It melts and becomes a part of the air, a part of everything." This is the attitude to life that we must attempt to adopt in order to appreciate the Inuit imagination. By using a surprising image, Papialook tells us that it is not possible to compartmentalize knowledge and experience. Everything is connected to everything else through unseen forces

11. Josiah Nuilaalik   Baker Lake 1991   *Flying Bear*
An angakoq has entered the spirit of the bear to journey to the spirit world. A flying bear helping spirit expressed the angakoq's mastery of the three elements.

almost as in a complex string game. Things as commonplace as the song of a bird or as seemingly humble as a name written on snow establish a connection to an invisible spirit world.

The Inuit believed that unseen forces governed every aspect of existence from birth to death. All living things and even inanimate objects were possessed by spirits or souls called *inua*. The word *inuk*, which is most often translated as man or person, is the possessive singular of *inua*. The plural form *inuit* is translated as the people, but, more significantly, an *inuk* is one possessed by a soul and the *Inuit* are those who have souls. After a long absence, the Polar Eskimo would greet one another with the question, "*Inussuarana*? Are you a spirit or a man?" The expected response was, "*Inussuanga*. I am a man."

Words themselves were believed to have great power, and the old beliefs are deeply embedded in the Inuit language, *inuktitut*, which means literally "to be as an inuk." Peter Freuchen recorded a fable describing the beginning of the world that indicates in a startling way the primary significance attached to words.

> In the beginning there was nothing but water. But then suddenly stones and rocks began to rain down from the sky. And land was created.
>
> But there was darkness, and animals and humans lived promiscuously among each other, copulating as they pleased, and assuming each other's shapes without order or reason.
>
> But in this blessed darkness words were born. And since words were new and never had been used before, they were as powerful as magic formulas. And strange things began to happen in the world because words were pronounced.

Because of the powers attributed to words, there were many taboos concerning the use of the names of animals and objects. On a journey, the name of a river or

12. Abraham Kingmiaqtuk   Spence Bay 1989   *Sea Spirit*
The angakoq's bear and walrus helping spirits assist him on the dangerous journey to the
spirit world.

mountain would not be spoken until it had been crossed over safely. Following the same principle, caribou were called "earth lice" and seals were called "sea lice" when they were hunted. Seals were also referred to as "the things that have blubber." A polar bear was "the great white one" or "the one without a shadow," and a caribou was "the animal with antlers." By avoiding their proper names, the spirits of these animals would not be offended. A bear seen in the distance would be called "one wearing the skin of a bear." Instead of saying that he was going out to hunt seals, a hunter would say that he was going out to try to get a hunting share.

A person's name was an essential part of his spirit or soul. A newborn child cried out with its first breath because it wanted a name. The name or name-spirit was taken from someone who had died and carried with it the qualities of those who had possessed it before. In many circumstances, it would be spoken with reluctance or a substitute name would be used to prevent the loss of its power. In his early years in the arctic, Peter Freuchen found it difficult to learn the names of the Inuit he met. They would say "*Oanga* (It is I)." When he asked again "But who are you?", they would repeat "*Oanga!*" This was particularly troublesome during the dark winter months. He eventually learned that a Polar Eskimo would never say his name since to do so could break its magic protection. Out of necessity, Freuchen trained himself to recognize everyone by voice alone. The Copper Eskimo observed by Diamond Jenness were not so concerned to avoid all mention of their names; "Unlike the Mackenzie and Alaskan natives, these Eskimos have no hesitation whatever in telling their own names; nor is there any taboo against mentioning the names of the dead, though the speaker will usually remark that the person referred to is dead and seems to expect that the matter will be dropped as having no further interest."

The act of breathing established a connection to Sila, the powerful spirit of the air that controlled the weather. The word *sila* could also mean simply the weather or the air or the world outside. *Silaaluk* or great Sila meant terrible weather. Jenness was told that Sila was a being who lived in the sky and made the sun go down as he walked along. This great spirit was often hostile to people but sometimes he would cure a sick man by imparting to him some of his own vitality. According to Rasmussen, *sila* conveyed the meaning of "a mixture of common sense, intelligence and wisdom." The phrase *silatuujuk* is translated "he is intelligent" but also means more directly "he is endowed with spirit or life-force." A person who died was said to have lost his breath. The famous custom of nose rubbing to show affection and also the unique throat singing both involve an exchange of breath. At a symbolic level, these customs express an acceptance of the essential nature of the other person. Significantly, the word *anirniq* is used to mean both breath and soul or spirit and is related to the word for making a song or poem. Raymond de Coccola noted that "Itireitok used the same word *anernek* to denote breath, soul and spirit, because her own soul was living and breathing, capable of surviving after death."

The natural world reflected the underlying spirit world. One time, Rasmussen admired the matchless spectacle when "the sun was low on the horizon, the sky and the land all around aglow with flaming colour." His travelling companion, the Caribou Eskimo Igjugarjuk, interpreted the scene for him. "A youth is dead and gone up into the sky, and the Great Spirit colours earth and sky with a joyful red to receive his soul." The aurora borealis arching brilliantly over the night sky had a spiritual significance. Lucien Turner recorded the belief that the northern lights were torches held by spirits seeking those who have just died in order to lead them along a narrow path to the land of brightness and plenty. These spirits could communicate with the living by making a whistling noise. The Inuit responded in a whispering tone, sending messages to the dead. In recent times, the writer Edith Iglauer was told of similar beliefs. "In Eskimo we call the northern lights Uksawnee. The Eskimo have a superstition that if you whistle and bang on something and make noise, the Uksawnee will reach down toward the person making noise. Eskimo children believe that if the Uksawnee touch you, you die. So ever since we were kids, it's a favourite game to rush out, whistle and make noise, and rush back inside again where the Uksawnee can't touch you. The scientists say you can't hear the Uksawnee, but lots of us have heard them. Did you?" Hesitating a moment, Iglauer answered that she was not sure.

13. Davidialuk Alasua Amittu   Povungnituk c. 1970   *Northern Lights*
Davidialuk represents the aurora borealis reaching down to earth in the form of a dog to remind the hunter of the presence of the spirits. Dogs were known to become unsettled when spirits were near and they always barked at the northern lights.

In the traditional way of life, the confrontation with the spirit world was not a children's game. There was a constant preoccupation to observe the practices and rituals that were believed to show respect to the inua of their ancestors, of the animals they hunted, of the weather and of the unseen spirits. Since their own survival depended on killing and eating animals that were believed to be very similar to people, they lived in perpetual fear of the animal spirits. Dressed in animal skins themselves, Inuit hunters were forced to challenge the spirits of their prey in an unending contest. If they were defeated in this struggle, they could lose their identity and turn into animals or spirits with no hope of return to the human world. Raymond de Coccola was puzzled by the practice he observed of hitting fish over the head with a stick after they had been pulled out of the water. At first he was told that the fish died more quickly that way. Observing the same practice, Diamond Jenness was told only that "it had always been their custom." After some persistence, de Coccola learned a more serious reason. "Fish have souls like all human beings. They have to be killed in a certain way, and they have to be killed at once, or they will speak evil words to the hunter. We fear the souls of the dead—human or animal, bird or fish—for they bring starvation, sickness and suffering. That's why we must obey the rules of taboo." Another time, he heard a song meant to be sung during fishing that expressed these beliefs.

> Fish, fish! Am I such a fool
> To let you talk to me? Aya, ya, ya, a
> You come from the bottom of the sea
> To tell evil things to young and old,

14. Simon Takkiruq   Gjoa Haven 1989   *Spirit Giving Birth*
When all the ancient rules were followed, the souls of the animals they killed would return in other animals to be taken again.

Children, men, and women, Aya, ya, ya, a
I'll not let you speak to me,
For I am but a young man still
Who does not have a woman. Aya, ya, ya, a

When an animal spoke to a man, it first pushed back the skin of its face to reveal a humanlike face. In northern Alaska, young men were told never to catch an unfamiliar animal to which they could not give a name. They believed that the animal might pull the skin of its head back like a parka hood and talk to them.

The many rules and restrictions that had evolved over the centuries were followed out of fear of the consequences of disobeying them. Transgressions in the human or natural world were thought to resonate in the spirit world. Jenness learned that long ago people in the Bathurst Inlet region had broken the taboo against cooking caribou meat on the ice. The ice had cracked up and everyone had drowned. It was feared that this would happen again if the taboo was violated. A captured seal would be given its first drink of fresh water. This was done to ensure that its spirit was pleased and would return in another seal to be taken again. There were prohibitions on hunting sea and land animals at the same time of the year. Caribou skin clothing could not be made when live caribou were near. Dogs were not allowed to gnaw caribou bones during the caribou hunting season or seal bones during the sealing season. Boys were not allowed to make string figures because it was feared that when they became men their fingers might become entangled in the harpoon line. At all times, there were strict rules governing the sharing of food with others. Many of these almost automatic practices have survived in some form until present times. Fred Bruemmer, the outstanding photographer of arctic wildlife, lived for half a year with Ekalun, an old hunter from Bathurst Inlet. Whenever Ekalun captured a seal, he would never fail to thank it profusely for permitting itself to be killed and thus providing them with food.

Some of the most important taboos governed birth and death. At these critical times, there was an increased danger of malevolent interference from the spirit world. Jenness was told that Mannigyorina had difficulty in delivering her child because the shades of the dead were angry. One belief was that a pregnant woman who violated the rules would be punished by having her child changed from a boy to a girl at the moment of birth. Women who had recently given birth were kept isolated for a time and allowed only a very restricted diet. There were many rituals that accompanied the birth of a child. Duncan Pryde saw the father of a newborn baby girl touch her mouth with the beak of a yellow-bellied loon. This was done to give the child a beautiful voice for the songs of the drum dance. The possessions of those who died could not be used by the living. It was believed that these possessions would attract the spirits of the departed to return with unpredictable consequences. The dead person was carried through the side of the igloo, which was then abandoned. The body was wrapped in seal or caribou skins with an opening at the mouth or above the head to enable the spirit to leave. The body was then enclosed in a ring of stones or covered with a mound of stones. The old woman Itireitok told de Coccola, "Departed souls can be so troublesome! I am afraid of them. It is no good for them to be wandering about,

15. Alasuaq Amittu Povungnituk 1982 *Totem*
A dream for a long night in winter. Living between the animal and spirit worlds and
depending on both, the people strived to keep everything in a precarious balance.

forlorn and unattached. That is why we name a dog after the dead person when no newborn child is in the family to receive that name."

Through amulets and magic words, every person was in some contact however tenuous with the spirit world. Lucien Turner observed that it was common to wear small images of the object or animal after which the person was named. The wearing of amulets (*atagtat* or "attachments") was universal since they were believed to confer some protection against evil spirits. The foot of a loon worn on a hunter's clothing would give skill in handling kayaks since loons were known to be strong swimmers. The head and claw of a raven would ensure a good share of food from hunting since the raven was always close by when animals were killed. The claw of a hawk worn as an amulet would give a good grip. The head, claws or skin of a falcon was believed to give courage because the falcon does not fear to attack birds bigger than itself. The ear of a caribou would confer good hearing and caribou sinew would give great strength. A wolf's paw would enable a hunter to become as hardy and enduring as a wolf. A ptarmigan skin would allow the hunter to be well camouflaged like the ptarmigan in its summer plumage. A fly would make its wearer invulnerable since flies were very difficult to capture.

The longer that an amulet was worn the greater its power became. Knud Rasmussen found little girls of five or six years old weighed down by numerous amulets intended to protect the sons that they would bear in the years to come. One young girl's collection included a swan's beak to ensure that her first child would be a boy, the head and foot of a ptarmigan to give the boy speed and endurance in hunting caribou, a bear's tooth to give powerful jaws and sound digestion, the pelt of an ermine to give strength and agility, and a little dried flounder as protection against dangerous encounters with strange tribes. The little Netsilik girl Qaqortigneq carried on her amulet belt the head of a grouse to make her sons swift, tireless runners and the head of an arctic hare to ensure a short and pretty nose. One small boy carried eighty amulets on his clothing as protections against all possible misfortunes.

In trading for these amulets, Rasmussen displayed considerable understanding of Inuit customs and some necessary diplomatic skills. He recognized that amulet hunting was a "delicate business" since it had to be done in such a manner that he would not be held responsible for any misfortunes that might happen to those who had given up their magic objects. When the visitors arrived, the Netsilik women marched around the sledges in a solemn procession designed to ward off any malevolent spirits that might have accompanied the outsiders. To overcome their concerns, Rasmussen explained that since he was a foreigner from across the wide seas, the rules governing Inuit life did not apply to him. He argued that "an owner of an amulet still enjoyed its protection even in the event of losing the amulet itself — and this was agreed." His arguments were persuasive in this small community. The next day he acquired several hundred amulets, giving in exchange such treasures as knives, needles, nails and matches. He also gave up pieces of an old shirt and, more reluctantly, some locks of his hair that were to serve as new amulets.

Magic words and songs were passed from father to son over many generations. There were songs that were believed to have been handed down from the

16. Anonymous Spence Bay c.1970 *Magic Words*
The shaman's songs come from the earliest times, when men and animals spoke to each other in the same language. The enlarged ears are a sign of transformation, and they represent the sensitivity of the angakoqs to everything around them.

"men of the first times." Some were sung with a slow monotonous melody, while others were spoken in a soft voice and repeated many times. If not spoken in the right way, they would lose their power. De Coccola recorded the magic words given to the hunter Kakagun by his father. "Wanderers of the Land, come, come and place your paws on this fresh snow!" These magic formulas were used at times of danger or crisis. They were employed to heal the sick, to end storms and to conjure animals to approach the hunters to be captured. The following song was used by the Labrador Eskimo during hunting.

> Today I am hunting for seals in the kayak.
> Come over here, all of you.
> (I am very cold.)
> You are not unwelcome,
> We are glad to see strangers.
> Where are you going?
> (I am very tired, I have walked from far.)
> What is that like deer far away?
> Today it rains again.

In the Igloolik area, there was a song that served the same purpose.

> Beast of the sea!
> Come and place yourself before me
> In the dear early morning!
> Beast of the plain!
> Come and place yourself before me
> In the dear early morning!

Another Igloolik song was designed to make travelling easier.

> I speak with the mouth of Qeqertuanaq and say:
> I will walk with leg muscles strong
> As the sinews on the shin of a little caribou calf.
> I will walk with leg muscles strong
> As the sinews on the shin of a little hare.
> I will take care not to walk toward the dark.
> I will walk toward the day.

This was one of the magic songs that Aua had obtained from Qeqertuanaq, an old woman whose family had handed them down from "the very first people on earth." To work their powers, these magic formulas had to be spoken in her name. As payment, Aua agreed to provide for Qeqertuanaq for the rest of her life.

Songs were considered to be private possessions and even a type of personal wealth. In times of need as in the case of Qeqertuanaq, they could be traded to others and they would then work their powers only for the new owners. According to Kaj Birket-Smith, "Every man has his own song, which he alone has the right to sing. These songs are often difficult for outsiders to grasp on account of their allusiveness; but in many cases they contain profound and impressive poetry." Complete faith in the power of words was believed by Rasmussen to be an essential requirement in the composition of magic words and songs.

> When I asked Ivaluardjuk about the power of words, he would smile shyly and
> answer that it was something no one could explain; for the rest, he would refer me

to the old magic song that I had already learned, and which made all difficult things easy. Or to the magic words which had power to stop the bleeding from a wound. "This is blood, that flowed from a piece of wood."

His idea in citing this example was to show that the singer's faith in the power of words should be so enormous that he should be capable of believing that a piece of dry wood could bleed, could shed warm red blood—wood, the driest thing there is.

Among the Copper Eskimo, Heq explained to Rasmussen, "the spirit hymns have to do with supernatural and unreal things so ordinary people do not need to understand them. The wisdom in them is concealed, and one must simply utter the words, which have a special power."

Rasmussen heard a very moving magic song that was recited by Aua to a newborn child to bring it good fortune through the difficult journey of life.

> I rise up from rest
> Moving swiftly as the raven's wing
> I rise up to meet the day — Wa — wa —
> My face is turned from the dark of night
> My gaze toward the dawn,
> Towards the whitening dawn.

Another of Aua's magic songs was intended for sick children.

> Little child!
> Your mother's breasts are full of milk.
> Go to her and suck,
> Go to her and drink.
> Go up into the mountain.
> From the mountain's top
> Shalt thou find health;
> From the mountain's top
> Shalt thou win life.

The old Polar Eskimo woman Simigaq shared her magic songs with Rasmussen the night before he set out on the Fourth Thule Expedition, a hazardous journey across the interior of Greenland. One she called the song of life, the song for one who wishes to live.

> Day arises
> From its sleep,
> Day wakes up
> With the dawning light
> Also you must arise,
> Also you must awake
> Together with the day which comes.

Simigaq said that her songs were poor and insignificant, a collection of short, meaningless words. "But what about that? After all, we humans understand so little of that which is met with in places where one is alone with the silent world."

**17. Isaac Panigayak
Gjoa Haven 1989 *Trance***
Symbolized by the exposed bone of one leg and the staring eyes at two levels, the angakoq is abandoning his human form. Later, he must find it again. In Siberian shamanism, shamans performed with one foot bare to remain in contact with the earth as the soul departed.

**18. Novoalia Alariaq
Cape Dorset c.1970
*Shaman's Body***
A sign of the angakoq's self control was the ability to manipulate the parts of his body. As in this sculpture, some angakoqs could remove their head or an arm and then replace it.

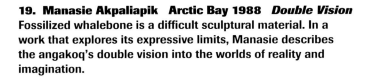

19. Manasie Akpaliapik   Arctic Bay 1988   *Double Vision*
Fossilized whalebone is a difficult sculptural material. In a work that explores its expressive limits, Manasie describes the angakoq's double vision into the worlds of reality and imagination.

20. Nick Sikkuark   Pelly Bay 1991   *Calling the Spirit*
Acting as a healer, the angakoq must find and call out all evil spirits. The sinew from a young caribou calf was a powerful amulet that symbolized strength.

Certain individuals had a special ability to communicate with the invisible forces. The shamans or *angakoqs* were men and women set apart from their communities by their spiritual powers, which were usually acquired after a difficult apprenticeship. The call to become a shaman was received with great reluctance and even with dread, so great was the fear of malevolent spirits. Parents warned their children not to remember the shaman's songs out of fear that they would acquire his powers. Signs that a person could become an angakoq might appear in vivid dreams. They might be indicated by unusual success in hunting or by unexplained skill in forecasting the weather. Seeing double images of objects was another indication that a young person could acquire the power to see into the spirit world. The second image was interpreted as the inua or soul of the object. A child that cried more than usual for no apparent reason was suspected to have the ability to communicate with the unseen spirits. According to Lucien Turner, "almost every person who can do anything not fully understood by others has more or less reputation as a shaman." The Copper Eskimo Ilatsiak had been seriously ill when he was a boy. Believing that there was no further hope, the angakoqs commanded him to go outside to die. When he recovered, it was clear that he was favoured by the spirits. Ilatsiak later became the most celebrated angakoq in the region.

On some occasions, individuals could acquire for a time the powers of an angakoq. Peter Freuchen noted that every year in the fall when the dark months began there seemed to be an epidemic of evil spirits. "Sometimes nerves would reach the limits of endurance, consciousness would be cancelled out and the individual in question would become senseless and hysterical, doing and saying

21. Johnassie Iqaluk   Sanikiluaq c.1955   *Angakoq*
"If it is generally true that most powerful shamans were well in control of their tornaqs (helping spirits), there were other tornaqs that were very independent. Such was the case with the spirit called Orpingalik, who used to attack his master Anaidjuq suddenly from behind and pull off his genitals; the unfortunate shaman, after much yelling, had to recover these in a trance" (Balikci 1970, 226). The reverse of the carving has the same outline as ancient ivory bear amulets.

22. John Kavik   Rankin Inlet c.1975   *Head*
A primitive carving that expresses the angakoq's concentration as he struggles to release his spirit.

incomprehensible things. However, the Eskimo regard this as a sacred state. The afflicted person is temporarily given the same respect as is shown the angakoq, and after his seizure he is invited to interpret what has been revealed to him. His revelations can sometimes be startling." It was believed that very few would dare to claim falsely to be an angakoq. A false shaman would live in fear of the inevitable, terrible retribution of the unseen powers. Kaj Birket-Smith heard from a Netsilik Eskimo of an angakoq who claimed that he could drive a harpoon through his body without leaving the smallest mark. Birket-Smith was surprised to learn that any "skepticism of the truth of such a narrative is met with complete incomprehension." He was asked, "Why doubt what the man said? Surely he knows best himself?" The Polar Eskimo shaman Saqdloq had the ability to crawl out of his skin and then to draw it back on. He had never been seen in this "flesh-bare" state since to do so would mean instant death.

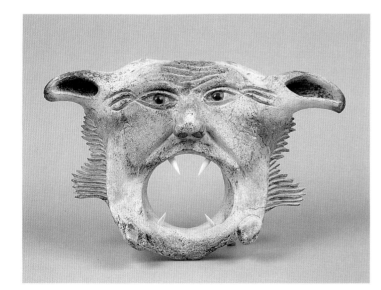

23. Manasie Akpaliapik   Arctic Bay 1989   *Angakoq*
A shaman has piercing eyes and extended ears to show heightened sensitivity, an open mouth to join his magic words to nature, and flowing hair to symbolize flight.

24. Tommy Ashevak   Spence Bay 1988   *Spirit*
The distorted face expresses the pain and fear of the shamanic transformation. The hole in the body represents an opening to the spirits.

25. William Anautalik   Baker Lake 1980
Skeletal Shaman
"Especially very late in the evening as the sun is setting when suddenly the shaman is half red with the light, half blue with the shadow, his shadow can dissociate itself from him and take on its own independent life and disappear into the twilight. At that point, the shaman can become transparent" (Butler 1977).

The angakoqs played the important role to preserve and interpret the ancient traditions. Their name derives from the word *anga,* which means "maternal uncle" or, more generally, "one who commands respect." Rasmussen described the first steps that a young man in the Igloolik area would take to learn the secrets of the angakoqs. First, he handed over some of his possessions to his experienced instructor. This was partly as payment for his instruction, but it also symbolized the willingness of the apprentice shaman to break with his former existence. A usual gift was a tent pole with a gull's wing attached, signifying that the novice angakoq desired to learn how to fly to the spirit world. In the secret language of the shamans, a tent pole was *napata*, "that which holds something upright." The Copper Eskimo Uloksak gave a number of caribou to his shaman teacher in Bathurst Inlet to obtain command over certain spirits, but this alone was not sufficient to become an angakoq. After his purchase of the helping spirits, he attempted to summon them to come to him when out hunting all alone.

> For a time none came. Then one day when he was alone on an island several appeared one after the other. They forbade him to eat any part of the stomach of the caribou, but to eat plenty of its brains; if he obeyed them in this respect they promised to attend him and bestow on him magical powers. After giving him these injunctions they knocked him roughly about and changed him into a white man. In this condition he returned to camp, where other shamans held a seance over him and restored him to his proper form.

According to Jenness, Uloksak survived the dangers of this unusual metamorphosis to become one of the most noted shamans in the country. Ilatsiak received his helping spirits in a similar way.

> He was fishing for tomcod, all alone, when a spirit first appeared to him. It resembled a young man in appearance, and was accompanied by other spirits, but these Ilatsiak could not see. He was terrified when it approached him, and asked whether he was going to die, but the spirit answered that he would live for many winters and reach old age before he died. It caught a tomcod and made him eat it, and the eating of this fish gave him magical power. The spirit accompanied him

26. Charlie Ugyuk   Spence Bay 1990   *Drummer*
The angakoq is suspended between the two worlds of reality and imagination.
When his spirit takes flight, his skeleton remains behind, representing his death to
the human world.

back to his camp, conversing with him, and giving him various injunctions; thus he was forbidden to eat the intestines of any animal, only the meat and the fat. The spirit disappeared as soon as they reached the camp.

In 1916 when he visited the camp of the Canadian Arctic Expedition, Ilatsiak chose Jenness as his associate in magic or his angakoq partner because he believed that the outsider was a shaman who had the power to change into any form he wished.

From 1902 to 1904, Rasmussen participated in the Danish Literary Expedition that studied the mythology of the Polar Eskimo and other Inuit groups in Greenland. He recorded a very literal translation of Otaq's account of his initiation as an angakoq. A young man about twenty-five years of age, Otaq (or Odark) was one of the best hunters among the Polar Eskimo.

> I wanted to become a magician, and go up to the hills, far into the hills and rocks, very far, and sleep up there. Up there I see two spirits, two were there, two great hill spirits, tall, as tall as a tent. They sang drum songs, they went on singing drum songs, the two great hill spirits. I did not utter one word; I kept silence while they sang drum songs; I was ashamed and did not dare to speak to them. The day after I went home; and then I was a little of a magician, only a very little of a magician.
>
> Another time I started out again on a little ramble in the hills, hare hunting, as I had felt a longing for hare's meat. A great rock I climbed up over, and when I came to the top I laid me down to sleep. I was not sleepy, but I just lay down. I lie there a little, lie and hear again the song of the hill spirits; it was the two great ones I had heard the last time. The one now begins to speak, speaks to me, asks me for a ladle of wood. I only heard that they sang and that they spoke to me; myself I said nothing.
>
> When I came down to men, neither did I tell this time what I had seen. But I carved a ladle of wood, a very beautiful ladle of wood, with no dirt upon it. The third time I heard the song of the hill spirits, I had not gone to the hills, that time it was in my house. Then they sought of themselves, then I was beginning to become a magician, more and more, but men knew nothing of it.
>
> When I saw the hill spirits again a great dog was running after them, a parti-coloured dog; it, too, became a helping spirit. It was only when many people fell sick that I revealed myself as a magician. And I helped many who were ill. My helping spirits know my thoughts and my will, and they help me when I give commands.

In this plain account, Otaq describes his acquisition of the basic tools of the angakoq, a collection of magic words and songs, the command of helping spirits, and the ability to enter at will the exalted dream-like state. Uncertain of his powers, he waits until misfortune strikes before he reveals himself as a shaman.

Through experiencing cold, hunger and solitude, by learning the secret shamanic language, and by repeating magic words and songs, the young person would acquire the spiritual powers of an angakoq. After a prolonged struggle, his helping spirits would appear in a personal revelation. In northern Alaska, the shaman teacher told his student, "I am going to take your life and give you the life of the angakoq." The Caribou Eskimo shaman Igjugarjuk told Rasmussen about this difficult transformation; "All true wisdom is only to be learned far from the dwellings of men, out in the great solitudes, and is only to be attained through suffering. Privation and suffering are the only things that can open the mind of man to those things which are hidden from others." His own initiation involved some extreme hardships.

> Igjugarjuk himself, when a young man, was constantly visited by dreams which he could not understand. Strange unknown beings came and spoke to him, and when he awoke, he saw all the visions of his dream so distinctly that he could tell his fellows all about them. Soon it became evident to all that he was destined to become an angakoq and an old man named Perqanaoq was appointed his instructor. In the depth of winter, when the cold was most severe, Igjugarjuk was placed on a small sledge just large enough for him to sit on, and carried far away from his home to the other side of Hikoligjuaq. On reaching the appointed spot, he remained seated on the sledge while his instructor built a tiny snow hut, with barely room for him to sit cross-legged. He was not allowed to set foot on the snow, but was lifted from the sledge and carried into the hut, where a piece of skin just large enough for him to sit on served as a carpet. No food or drink was given him; he was exhorted to think only of the Great Spirit and of the helping spirit that should presently appear — and so he was left to himself and his meditations.
>
> After five days had elapsed, the instructor brought him a drink of lukewarm water, and with similar exhortations, left him as before. He fasted now for fifteen days, when he was given another drink of water and a very small piece of meat, which had to last him for a further ten days. At the end of this period, his instructor came for him and fetched him home. Igjugarjuk declared that the strain of those thirty days of cold and fasting was so severe that he "sometimes died a little." During all that time he thought only of the Great Spirit, and endeavoured to keep his mind free from all memory of human beings and everyday things. Towards the end of the thirty days there came to him a helping spirit in the shape of a woman. She came while he was asleep, and seemed to hover in the air above him. After that he dreamed no more of her, but she became his helping spirit.

Hikoligjuaq, "the great water with ice that never melts," was a significant choice as the site of the novice shaman's ordeal. Since time immemorial, the shores of this lake had served as a meeting place in the spring for the peoples of the Barren Lands and their neighbours to the west and north.

The well-being of the community was believed to depend on the powers of their angakoq. Until they had demonstrated their abilities, novice shamans were viewed very skeptically. Diamond Jenness observed a seance performed by Agluak, a young man whose shamanistic powers were not regarded very seriously. "He had dropped his mittens during the seance, and was looking around for them when it was over; someone at the back of the hut threw them into his face, causing a general laugh. The women resented his prohibition against sewing [to enable the men to have good luck again in their sealing] and for the most part disregarded it." The acceptance of a young person as a new angakoq was an important collective decision that was symbolized by the gift of a special belt, as recorded by Rasmussen.

> As soon as a young man has become a shaman, he must have a special shaman's belt as a sign of his dignity. This consists of a strip of hide to which are attached

many fringes of caribou skin, and these are fastened on by all the people he knows, as many as he can get; to the fringes are added small carvings, human figures made of bone, fishes, harpoons; all these must be gifts, and the givers then believe that the shaman's helping spirits will always be able to recognize them by their gifts, and will never do them any harm.

The use of the angakoq's belt to heal sick people was observed by the Anglican missionary Donald Marsh in the Keewatin region. "The angakoq would take a piece of cloth or animal skin from the patient, tear it in half, return half to the patient and wear the other half as his or her own, thus taking away the sickness from the patient." Rasmussen acquired a shaman's belt from Kinalik, an angakoq who had been instructed by Igjugarjuk.

> It consisted of an ordinary strap of hide on which were hung or strung the following items: a splinter from the stock of a gun in recognition of the fact that her initiation had taken place by means of visions of death; a piece of sinew thread, which had formerly been used to fasten tent poles with, and had on some occasion or other been used for a magic demonstration; a piece of ribbon from a packet of tobacco; a piece of an old cap formerly belonging to her brother—the brother was now dead, and was one of her helping spirits—a piece of white caribou skin, some plaited withies [twigs], a model of a canoe, a caribou's tooth, a mitten and a scrap of sealskin. All these things possessed magnetic power, by virtue of their having been given to her by persons who wished her well. Any gift conveys strength. It need not be great or costly in itself; the intrinsic value of the object is nothing, it is the thought which goes with it that gives strength.

To gain her powers as an angakoq, Kinalik had been suspended in midwinter from tent poles planted in the snow. At a time of intense cold, she was left there for five days, but the spirits protected her. When she was finally taken down, her instructor Igjugarjuk was asked to shoot her so that visions of death would bring her into contact with the spirit world. Instead of a lead bullet, a stone was used so that she would remain in contact with the earth. When she was shot, Kinalik fell to the ground but revived the next day with no apparent harm.

Before Rasmussen and his companions left this small group of Caribou Eskimo, a song festival was held in their honour. Kinalik volunteered to call upon her helping spirits to clear the way ahead for them.

> All the singing now ceased, and Kinalik stood forth alone with her eyes tightly closed. She uttered no incantation but stood trembling all over, and her face twitched from time to time as if in pain. This was her way of "looking inward" and penetrating the veil of the future; the great thing was to concentrate all one's forces intently on the one idea, of calling forth good for those about to set out on their journey. . . . When Kinalik had reached the utmost limit of her concentration, I was requested to go outside the tent and stand on the spot where there were no footmarks, remaining there until I was called in. Here, on the untrodden snow, I was to present myself before Sila, standing silent and humble, and desiring sky and air and all the forces of nature to look upon me and show me goodwill.

Apparently the divination was successful. When Rasmussen was called into the tent, Kinalik was her normal self again. She told him that the Great Spirit had

27. Esa Qillaq   Clyde River 1987   *Soul Flight*
Calling on his animal helping spirits, the shaman's soul takes flight to the spirit world.
The upraised arms symbolize both flight and the humanity of the angakoq.

28. **Nelson Takkiruq   Gjoa Haven 1989   *Shaman Drummer***

29. **George Tataniq   Baker Lake c. 1970**

30. **Joseph Suqslak   Gjoa Haven 1990**

31. **Mark Tootiak   Gjoa Haven 1982**

32. **Davie Atchealak   Pangnirtung 1988**

33. **Edward Snowball   Kangisualujjuaq 1986**

34. **Emily Illuitok   Pelly Bay 1992**

The hypnotic beat of the qilaut, the caribou skin drum, allows the angakoq to enter an ecstatic trance state to begin the visionary journey. Aided by walrus, bear and bird helping spirits and the amulets suspended from his belt, the shaman's soul takes flight to the spirit world.

35. Josiah Nuilaalik   Baker Lake 1992 *Hunting for Walrus*
When hunting walrus or seal, the head of the first animal taken was displayed on the kayak. This frightened the other animals and they would flee towards the hunters lying in wait for them. The sea mammals feared the bear even more than they feared the human hunters.

heard her prayer. All dangers would be removed from the paths of the travellers.

Among the Copper Eskimo of the western arctic, the angakoq was known as *elik*, which means literally "the one who has eyes." In the Igloolik area, the aspiring shaman would say to his teacher, "I come to you because I desire to see." The shamanic term for a person who sees something supernatural was *takunamiktoq*, "one who gets something in his eyes." The shaman, unlike normal people, had the ability to see into the spirit world, to see into darkness and to see far away. This gift of sight was used to cure illness, to help a barren woman to have a child, to end periods of bad weather and to ensure good hunting at times of hunger and famine. The shaman's equipment consisted of little more than the belt or necklace from which the amulets were suspended and perhaps a simple headband or a headdress in the shape of the head of a bear, raven or loon. Jenness observed that "the Copper Eskimo shaman, whether man or woman, had no distinctive mark or dress of any kind, not even during the seances." The large caribou skin drum used to accompany their song and dance performances was also used in the shamanic rituals. The drum was called *qilaut*, which means "that which helps to call up the spirits."

When his powers were needed, the angakoq would go into a hypnotic trance produced by intense concentration or by the rhythmic beat of the qilaut and the chanting of a repetitive song. Once in the trance, the angakoq was believed to leave the world of the living to travel to the spirit world. Leaving his body behind, he would call on his helping spirits to guide him in this journey and to help him overcome the many dangers. He might travel to the moon to visit the kindly moon spirit Tarqeq or to the bottom of the sea to visit Sedna, the mother of the sea creatures. When he reached his destination in the spirit world, he would attempt to learn the causes of the community's misfortunes. He would discover that some taboos had been violated, offending some of the spirits. Returning from this unearthly world, he would again need his skill and his spirit helpers to find his way back to the living. There he would give a vivid account of his dangerous journey and rebuke those who had broken the taboos.

The healing ritual of the angakoq had many similarities to an unrehearsed theatrical performance. The shaman diverted the dangers afflicting individuals and the community onto himself, undergoing a type of death and resurrection. In the ritual, there was an essential mutual interaction between the angakoq and the onlookers, in which all the participants understood their roles. Depending on the strength of their mutual involvement, the shaman's trance could be extended to last several hours or longer to the point of emotional and physical exhaustion of all present. In the performance, there could be unexpected visits from the spirit world and there might be a flow of questions and answers addressed to the spirits. Franz Boas described one of these shamanic performances designed to learn the cause of an illness.

> The lamps being lowered, the angakoq strips off his outer jacket, pulls the hood over his head, and sits down in the back part of the hut facing the wall. He claps his hands, which are covered with mittens, and shaking his whole body, utters sounds which one would hardly recognize as human.
>
> Thus he evokes his *tornaq* (helping spirit), singing and shouting, alternately, the listeners, who sit on the edge of the bed, joining the chorus and answering his questions. Then he asks the sick person: "Did you work when it was forbidden? Did you eat when you were not allowed to eat?" And if the poor fellow happens to remember any transgression of such laws, he cries: "Yes, I have worked. Yes, I have eaten." And the angakoq rejoins "I thought so" and issues commands as to the manner of atonement.

36. Kiawak Ashoona
Cape Dorset 1991   *Bird Shaman*

37. Josiah Nuilaalik   Baker Lake 1990
Bird Shaman

Images of the shaman's abandonment of his human personality on the soul journey to the spirit world.

38. Anonymous   Cape Dorset c. 1968   *Half-bird, Half-fish*
39. Philip Pitseolak   Pond Inlet c. 1965   *Sea Spirit*

Visualizations of the creatures that appear in dreams and the imagination.

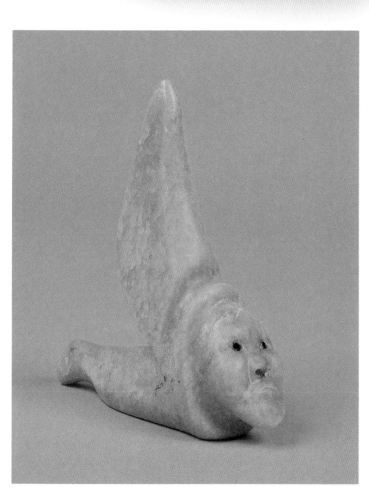

40. Gideon Qauqjuaq   Spence Bay c. 1980   *Parka Wing*
The parka hood is turning into a wing.

41. Maudie Rachel Okittuq   Spence Bay 1991
Spirit Transformation
The distorted proportions of the part-human, part-animal figure indicate the angakoq's transformation.

42. Judas Ullulaq Gjoa Haven 1988
Muskox Shaman
Muskox horns are symbols of strength, courage and permanence. The angakoq has been released from his body. Only the tattoos remain to show the spirits that he is flesh and blood.

43. Paul Toolooktook
Baker Lake 1991 *Walrus Shaman*
"A whaling master once told me that he had watched a shaman at close range 'grow' a set of walrus tusks. So cleverly was this feat performed that the whaler was unable to understand how it had been done" (Copland, 21).

44. Maudie Rachel Okittuq   Spence Bay c. 1980   *Healing*
An angakoq attempts to draw out the evil spirit and call back the soul that has wandered
from the body of the sick man. A bird looks on, indicating the presence of the spirits.

To reinforce the belief in their powers, the angakoqs were not above using simple or elaborate conjuring tricks. They were skilled ventriloquists and were able to mimic animal voices. They knew how to cast frightening shadows resembling grotesque animals or spirits on the walls of the igloo. At the climax of a healing performance, they would appear to draw a small animal from the body of the sick person. In the annual festival in honour of the powerful sea spirit Sedna, the angakoq would appear to be fatally harpooned and then would recover miraculously. Boas reported a shaman's performance observed on Baffin Island in the winter of 1886–87.

> An angakoq began his incantations in a hut after the lamps were lowered. Suddenly he jumped up and rushed out of the hut to where a mounted harpoon was standing. He threw himself upon the harpoon, which penetrated his breast and came out at the back. Three men followed him and holding the harpoon line led the angakoq, bleeding profusely, to all the huts of the village. When they arrived again at the first hut he pulled out the harpoon, lay down on the bed, and was put to sleep by the songs of another angakoq. When he awoke after a while he showed to the people that he was not hurt, although his clothing was torn and they had seen him bleeding.

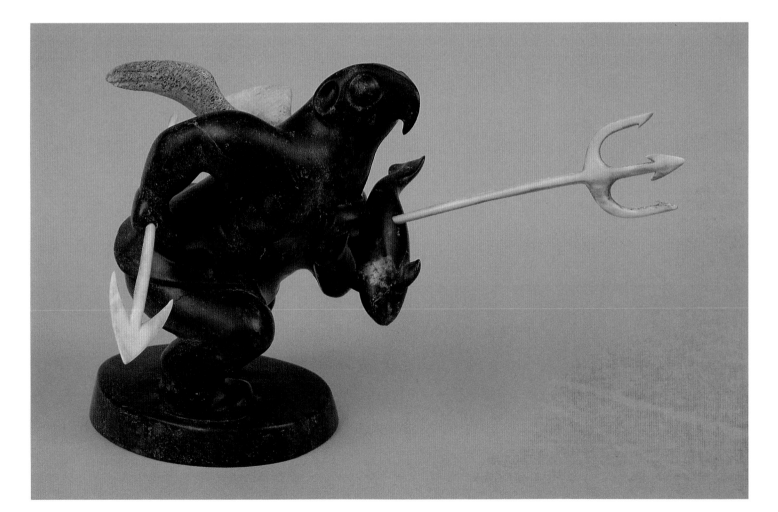

45. Charlie Ugyuk   Spence Bay 1988   *Helping Spirit*
The hunter calls on his bird helping spirit to give him the keen eyes and the patience of the birds when they are looking for fish.

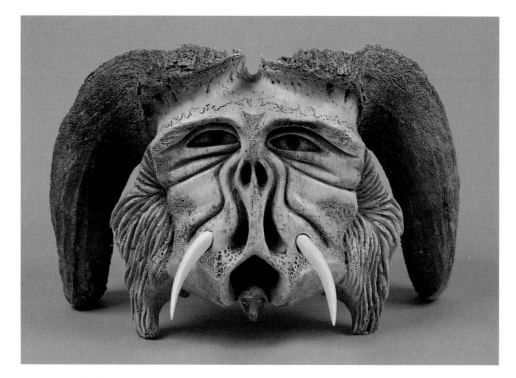

46. Manasie Akpaliapik   Arctic Bay 1988   *Muskox Shaman*
The angakoq is lost to the human world in the shamanic trance. Muskox horns are
permanent, a sign of the power of the muskox helping spirit.

The shamanic performances must have had a very dramatic effect in a claustrophobic atmosphere of excitement approaching hysteria. There was a strong will to believe in the powers of the angakoqs since otherwise there was no protection against the unseen forces. Although their powers could be abused, there was usually a benign purpose to the deceptions practised by the angakoqs. Their performances were designed to give hope to a people pursued by cold, sickness and hunger, a people who lived in constant fear of the incomprehensible forces of nature. And in most cases it was not deception. The belief was sincere. As Boas records, "the angakut themselves believe in their performances, as by continued shouting and invoking they fall into an ecstasy and really imagine they accomplish the flights and see the spirits." Diamond Jenness believed that the shamans were not conscious of acting a part, but instead in their minds they became the spirits that were believed to possess them. "To his audience, too, this strange figure, with its wild and frenzied appearance, its ventriloquistic cries and its unearthly falsetto gabble, with only a broken word here and there of intelligible speech, is no longer a human being, but the thing it personifies. Their minds become receptive of the wildest imaginings, and they see the strangest and most fantastic happenings."

Rasmussen was well aware of the deceptions practised by the angakoqs, writing that they may resort to the most transparent trickwork and yet be thoroughly in earnest. As a critical observer, he was never able to hear the rushing of mighty wings that accompanied the spirit flights in the old stories. The manifestations of spiritual powers that he witnessed were always disappointing to him. One time, he observed a young angakoq, Anarqaoq, seize an opportunity to demonstrate his powers. A crying child was not able to explain the source of his

47. David Ruben Piqtoukun Paulatuk, Toronto 1991
Bear Shaman
The bear is the most human of all the animals. At home on land
and in the sea, the one without a shadow was the most powerful
helping spirit.

48. George Arluk   Arviat c. 1970   *Muskox Spirit*
Before the rifle, the muskox was difficult to hunt. They never abandon their young,
guarding them until the end. The muskox helping spirit was very powerful.

complaint. The angakoq dashed out of the igloo and returned with his clothing torn and covered with blood after having fought with the evil spirits troubling the child. Anarqaoq had gained his reputation as a shaman by his reports of the fantastic spirit creatures that he saw in his dreams and when awake. Rasmussen asked him to draw his visions with pencil and paper. "After some hesitation he complied. And I could not but feel that he was himself convinced of their reality; he did not simply sit down and draw the things at once, but would remain for some time manifestly under the influence of strong emotion, trembling to such a degree that he could hardly draw at all."

According to Kaj Birket-Smith, the practice of shamanism was found in its simplest form among the Caribou Eskimo, the inland people of the Barren Grounds. To ponder a question, "the shaman retires into solitude where *Silap-inua* [the spirit of Sila] can notice him, and there he walks and walks, exhausted and fasting, in every kind of weather, thinking only of the matter in hand until his familiar spirit gives him an answer." In contrast to the "salt-water Eskimo," Igjugarjuk proudly told Rasmussen, their angakoqs did not dance about doing tricks and never spoke incomprehensibly. In their performances, "the one essential was truth and earnestness." Birket-Smith recorded a memorable account of a shamanic performance given by Igjugarjuk on the shore of great Hikoligjuaq, the scene of his initiation years before. The whole population gathered for the ceremony in a large caribou skin tent.

> In accordance with the usual practice, they began with song; for before the mystic rite can begin the minds of the company must be tuned to a festive mood. One by

49. Solomonie Tigullaraq   Clyde River c.1968 *Angakoq Bear*
An unusual vision of a sedentary helping bear spirit with the angakoq facing backward away from the spirit domain.

50. Thomas Sivuraq   Baker Lake 1991   *Bird Shaman*
The shamanic transformation when the angakoq's soul enters the spirit of the bird. The
boot and mitten are signs of the shaman's humanity.

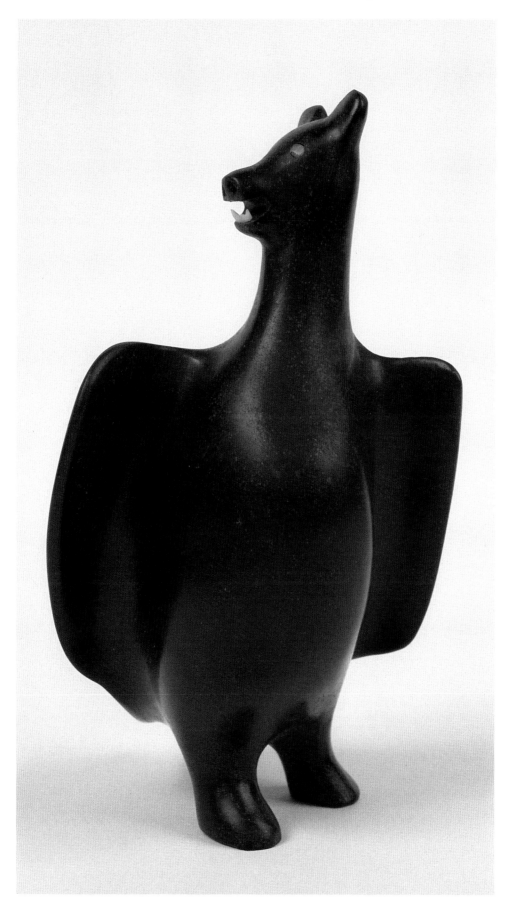

51. Josiah Nuilaalik Baker Lake 1991 *Bear Shaman*
"I don't know very much about shamans....I don't like to think about them...but my family
and my mother's family all believed in shamans because we had heard so many stories"
(Pitseolak Ashoona interviewed by Eber, 1977).

52. Kaka Ashoona   Cape Dorset 1991   *Spirit Head*
The stylized hair on the spirit head is a reminder that grooming the hair was a way to
show affection between people. It was also a way to keep the spirits pleased.

53. Henry Napartuk   Kuujjuaraapik c. 1970   *Seal Spirit*
A seal with a human head representing the inua of the animal.

54. Karoo Ashevak   Spence Bay c. 1965   *Angakoq*
A powerful head that indicates the intensity of the shamanic experience.

one the singers stepped forward. . . . At last came Igjugarjuk's turn. Each person had to press his hand, the women with the left, the men with the right hand. Even the sleeping children were roused and drowsily stretched out their little fists. Before him he placed one of his mittens, then wound his belt tightly round the point of his shaman's wand, a stick of wood, about half a yard long, 'brought from far away.' Now he touched the mitten with the wand, moving it slowly up and down. . . . Soon it seemed as if an invisible force was holding down the wand. With greater and ever greater difficulty he raised it, the orbit described becoming shorter and shorter, and the sweat stood out on his brow in great beads. The miracle had happened! There, just below us, down in the ground, was his familiar spirit answering the questions, yes or no, according to whether the wand could be lifted or not.

In the meantime the general conversation had died away. Only now and then was the stillness broken by a subdued call to the spirit: atê, atê! The atmosphere of uncertainty and tension was oppressive. The performance was repeated several times, until Igjugarjuk had interpreted the answers and announced the result. His voice was breathless and strained; there was no doubt that he himself firmly believed.

The ceremony concluded with handshaking again but this time with the hands crossed, some further singing for a short time, and finally everybody drank tea. The visitor then turned his attention to the wider scene, which seemed to reflect the calm that had come over the participants. "In the meantime the brief night had come to an end, and when at last we lay down to rest, the sun was about to rise over the low ridges in the northeast, and Hikoligjuaq's field of ice lay before us reflecting delicate tones of rose against a background of fantastic violet banks of cloud."

3. Sedna and the Shaman's Journey

A T T H E C O R E of the Inuit system of beliefs was the myth of Sedna, of a young girl who after a series of tragic events undergoes a supernatural metamorphosis to become the mother of the sea animals. Together with Sila, the spirit of the air and wind, and Tarqeq, the moon spirit, Sedna was believed to be one of the primal forces of nature. Her name has been translated as "the one who is before," indicating her primary importance. She was known by many names in different regions of the Inuit world. These included Nuliajuk, the poor wife; Niviarsiang, the girl; Kavna, she down there; Takanakapsaluk, the terrible one down there; Arnakapfaluk, the big woman; Uinigumissuitung, she who never wished to marry; Aivilayoq, she who gives useful things; and many other names. In the Inuit mythological framework, Sedna personified both the tragedies of life and the mysteries of creation. Her great power came from her control of the sea animals on which the people depended for their survival.

Every close observer of traditional Inuit life soon became aware of how this powerful spirit dominated almost every activity. When asked by Rasmussen to explain his beliefs, the old Caribou Eskimo hunter Ikinilik told him, "We do not believe, we only fear. And most of all we fear Nuliajuk." When Rasmussen then asked who was this deity and why did they fear her, many in the igloo attempted to answer. Every child knew her story and all were eager to tell it. It was Ikinilik who answered. "Nuliajuk is the name we give to the Mother of Beasts. All the game we hunt comes from her; from her comes all the caribou, all the foxes, the birds and fishes."

Success or failure in hunting depended on the unpredictable moods of this unseen power The Copper Eskimo shaman Horqarnaq attempted to summon the Mother of the Sea Beasts to bring calm weather so that the hunters could find food the next day for their children.

> Woman, great woman down there,
> Send it hence, send it away from us, that evil!
> Come, come spirit of the deep!
> One of your earth-dwellers
> Calls to you,
> Asks you bite enemies to death.
> Come, come, spirit of the deep!

The Netsilik angakoq Orpingalik told Rasmussen a magic song designed to induce the mother of all the sea animals to give up one of her offspring.

> O father- and motherless,
> O dear little-one-all-alone,
> Give me

Boots of caribou.
Bring me a gift,
A beast of those beasts
That make luscious blood soup;
A beast of the beasts
From the depths of the sea
And not from the plains of the earth.
Little father- and motherless one,
Bring me a gift.

The hunter Kudnanuk described to Raymond de Coccola the results of a recent fishing expedition. At first, Kudnanuk and his father had no success and they guessed at the reason. "Father and I thought we had offended Nuliajuk, so we hung ptarmigan's feet on our weasel fur parkas that night. The spirit mother of all animals was good to us after that." Another time after a bountiful dinner of seal meat, de Coccola was told, "Arnakapfaluk, the great woman Spirit of the Sea, has been good to us. But we don't know how long she will be pleased with us. We don't have Anilianaher, the shaman, to tell us if we have disobeyed the rules. Misfortune may come to us at any time."

Many of the rules and taboos governing Inuit life were followed to please Sedna. Nearing the birth of her child, Angivrana told de Coccola that she craved raw meat during the day. Despite her strong desire for meat, she was compelled to abstain. The local angakoq Kirluayok had decreed that she could eat only in the morning and evening. She explained why she had to obey. "Otherwise bad luck will befall me. The Big Woman Arnakapfaluk, the Spirit of the Sea, would bring misfortune to us all." To protect herself and the unborn child from evil

55. Makusikalla Aliqu Qullialu   Akulivik 1979 *Sedna and Young*
A maternal image of a peaceful Sedna.

56. Matiusi Luuku Ivujivik 1978 *Storm*
The bird husband pleaded for Sedna to return and caused a great storm by beating his wings. To save himself, the father threw his daughter into the sea. When she held on to the boat, her father cut off her hands joint by joint. Falling into the water, they became the sea mammals. The father then struck her with an oar, plucking out an eye. Sedna was transformed into a sea spirit.

57. Samson Kingalik Inukjuak 1979 *Abduction*
Living unhappily with her father, a young girl listens to the promises of a handsome man in fine clothes with a strong kayak. She discovers that he is not a man but a bird. He will not allow her to return to live with her people.

spirits when labour began, she wore caribou and seal-skin satchels slung over her belt. As the contractions increased, she called out for help from the spirits of her long dead father and grandmother. Despite all these precautions, her fears proved to be justified. When the child was born, Angivrana shouted in anguish, "It's too bad, too bad! It's only a girl!"

Sedna's story was told in many ways from the briefest accounts for children lasting perhaps a few minutes to lengthy versions that would have taken hours or several evenings to perform. The details varied considerably from one region to another, but the essentials of the story were similar. Rasmussen recorded a very clear account of the Sedna myth as it was told in the Igloolik region.

A girl would not have a husband, and at last her father in anger said that she would have his dog. One night then, the dog came in and took her to wife. When the girl became pregnant, the father isolated her on a small island, but the dog swam over to join her. It would swim in from time to time with the pack saddle to get meat from the father. The girl bore a litter — some dog children, some children in human form. Feeling sorry for her, the father one day loaded the dog with stones, concealed by meat on top. When the dog swam out, he sank and drowned. Then the father used to take the meat over to the island.

Next the angry daughter told her dog children to attack their grandfather's kayak, but he managed to escape back to the mainland. He dared not go to the island anymore. Now in want, the girl put her dog children in a boot sole setting three straws for masts, and they drifted out to sea to become the ancestors of the white men. She put her human form children in the additional outer sole of a boot and sent them drifting to the land to give rise to the Chipewyan Indians. Then she returned home to live with her parents once more.

One day while the father was away hunting, a kayak arrived and a fine big man called the girl out to go off with him; this she did. Stopping by an ice floe

58. Annie Qimirpik Lake Harbour 1978 *Possession*
Dreaming of a life without hardships, Sedna listened to the
entreaties of a handsome stranger. A second interpretation of
this work is that it represents a Christian image of demonic
possession.

59. Luke Arngna'naaq Baker Lake 1990 *Sedna's Anger*
As a sign of her rage, Sedna's hair flows loose and dishevelled
behind her. Unless her anger is appeased, terrible storms and
famine will ensue.

en route, the kayaker got out and removed his sun goggles, whereupon the girl
burst into tears for the man was puny, having only been sitting tall on a high seat,
and had ugly eyes, a northern fulmar in human form. They went on to the bird's
sealskin tent where they lived together and had a child.

But her sorrowing father set out in a boat to look for her and arrived one day
while the fulmar was out hunting. He took her away in his boat. The fulmar, in
bird form, caught up and swooping close it raised such a storm with its wings that
the boat nearly upset. In fear the father threw the girl overboard to her husband,
but she clung to the gunwale. So he chopped off her first finger joints, and they
bobbed up in the water as small seals. Again she grasped the boat's edge, so the
father hacked off the next finger joints which became bearded seals. Still the girl
hung on, and the last joints were cut off, forming the walrus. She sank then to
become a spirit, the mother of the sea beasts. The father got home, but in remorse
he lay down at the water's edge under a skin, and the tide swept him out to join his
daughter and the dog in a house at the bottom of the sea.

This account is the bare skeleton of the famous story. The storyteller would
expand some details and omit others to make his points or to catch the mood of
the moment. By marrying his daughter to his dog, Sedna's father expresses his
great anger and contempt for her behaviour. Because they lived in such a close
relationship with people, dogs were commonly believed to have no souls of their
own and no spirit powers. When she rejects all human suitors, Sedna puts herself outside the protection of both the normal human world and the spirit world.

The surprising references to the white men and the Chipewyan Indians are
evidently late additions to the ancient myth, or they may refer to early contacts

64. Gideon Qauqjuaq   Spence Bay c. 1975   *Angry Sedna*
"We fear Sedna's anger. That is why we follow the many rules that our angakoqs say will please her."

**60. Maudie Rachel Okittuq
Spence Bay 1990   *Sedna***
A personal visualization of the powerful sea spirit.

61. Saila Pudlat   Cape Dorset 1988   *Birth*
The Sedna myth centres on the mysteries of birth and creation. By following her rules, the spirits of the sea mammals will be born again and return to be caught again.

**62. David Ruben Piqtoukun
Paulatuk, Toronto 1990   *Angakoq Bear***
The shaman is hunting as a bear, the great white one who is equally powerful on the land and in the sea.

**63. Natar Ungalaq   Igloolik 1982
*Engraved Seal***
A seal is never simply a seal. The angakoq with walrus tusks has travelled to visit Sedna to ask her to release her children to the people above. During the drum dance, the people celebrate the success of the hunters.

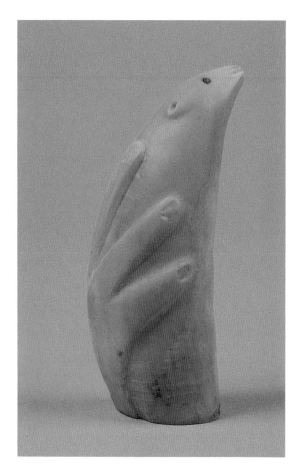

65. Bibiana Ittimangnaq   Pelly Bay c. 1970
Hand and Bear
A representation of the creation of the bear from Sedna's hand or a sign of the angakoq's control of the most powerful helping spirit.

with the Adlet (Indians). The Igloolik Inuit believed that the island in the story was nearby Tern Island, while the Greenlanders travelling with the Fifth Thule Expedition insisted that the events had occurred at Inglefield Gulf in the land of the Polar Eskimo. The argument of the visitors from Greenland was accepted as more convincing when they said that they had seen the grave of the dog there. Images from the Sedna legend were invoked constantly as metaphors in daily life. When de Coccola made a clumsy attempt to reproduce the string figure of a couple dancing, he was told that it looked like a dog's testicles. The Polar Eskimos obtained iron for their knives and harpoons from three large meteors near Thule that they called the dog, the woman and the tent. Among the Copper Eskimo, Diamond Jenness observed a revealing incident; "Whenever her dog was nosing about the house Higilak would cry in a high-pitched, ironically-seductive tone *arnennoak*, 'girl,' and the dog would slink out of doors again."

The more archaic Baffin Island version related by Franz Boas had been handed down in an old song. It contains many interesting differences, concentrating on the second half of the Igloolik story.

Once upon a time there lived on a solitary shore an Inung with his daughter Sedna. His wife had been dead for some time and the two led a quiet life. Sedna grew up to be a handsome girl and the youths came from all around to sue for her hand, but none of them could touch her proud heart. Finally, at the breaking up of the ice in the spring a fulmar flew from over the ice and wooed Sedna with enticing song. "Come to me," it said; "come into the land of the birds, where there is never hunger, where my tent is made of the most beautiful skins. You shall rest on soft bearskins. My fellows, the fulmars, shall bring you all your heart may desire; their feathers shall clothe you; your lamp shall always be filled with oil, your pot with meat." Sedna could not long resist such wooing and they went together over the vast sea. When at last they reached the country of the fulmar, after a long and hard journey, Sedna discovered that her spouse had shamefully deceived her. Her new home was not built of beautiful pelts, but was covered with wretched fish-skins, full of holes, that gave free entrance to wind and snow. Instead of soft reindeer skins her bed was made of hard walrus hides and she had to live on miserable fish, which the birds brought her. Too soon she discovered that she had thrown away her opportunities when in her foolish pride she had rejected the Inuit youth. In her woe she sang: "Aja. O father, if you knew how wretched I am you would come to me and we would hurry away in your boat over the waters. The birds look unkindly upon me the stranger; cold winds roar about my bed; they give me but miserable food. O come and take me back home. Aja."

When a year had passed and the sea was again stirred by warmer winds, the father left his country to visit Sedna. His daughter greeted him joyfully and besought him to take her back home. The father hearing of the outrages wrought upon his daughter determined upon revenge. He killed the fulmar, took Sedna into his boat, and they quickly left the country which had brought so much sorrow to Sedna. When the other fulmars came home and found their companion dead and his wife gone, they all flew away in search of the fugitives. They were very sad over the death of their poor murdered comrade and continue to mourn and cry until this day.

Having flown a short distance they discerned the boat and stirred up a heavy storm. The sea rose in immense waves that threatened the pair with destruction. In this mortal peril the father determined to offer Sedna to the birds and flung her overboard. She clung to the edge of the boat with a death grip. The cruel father then took a knife and cut off the first joints of her fingers. Falling into the sea they were transformed into whales, the nails turning into whalebone. Sedna holding on to the boat more tightly, the second finger joints fell under the sharp knife and swam away as seals; when the father cut off the stumps of her fingers they became ground seals. Meantime the storm subsided, for the fulmars thought Sedna was drowned. The father then allowed her to come into the boat again. But from that time she cherished a deadly hatred against him and swore bitter revenge. After they got ashore, she called her dogs and let them gnaw off the feet and hands of

66. Nellie Nuktie Kuujjuaraapik 1978 *Sedna's Home*
Sedna's desire to live in an imagined world has led to an unhappy existence in the realm of clams and sea urchins.

67. Emma Aola Arctic Bay 1974 *Creation*
A small sculpture that represents the great theme of creation.
The hand is mysteriously transforming into a whale.

68. Rosa Arnarudluk Kanayok Repulse Bay c. 1975
Lonely Sedna
A simple carving from walrus ivory that expresses the sorrow
and isolation of Sedna's existence.

69. Egesiak Peter Cape Dorset 1987 *Sedna Rising*
A visualization of the woman below rising from the bottom of the
sea to rejoin the human world.

her father while he was asleep. Upon this he cursed himself, his daughter, and the
dogs which had maimed him; whereupon the earth opened and swallowed the
hut, the father, the daughter, and the dogs. They have since lived in the land of
Adlivun, of which Sedna is the mistress.

The power of the myth of Sedna came from the fact that it raises the pro-
foundest fears of Inuit life. This gave the story an unbreakable hold on the imagination in the traditional culture. One fear was the fear of the elements, the cold
unfathomable sea from which they earned their precarious existence and the
wind with the terrible storms that it brings. Another was the fear of the animal
world with the danger of the loss of human identity. The myth confronts the primal fears of hunger, cold and mutilation. Perhaps the greatest fear was the fear of
separation from family, community and the human world. The tragedy centres

70. Abraham Etungat   Cape Dorset 1987   *Bird of Spring*
"We rejoice to see the proud birds return in spring to their nesting places. Winter is over and the carefree days of summer are almost here."

on two universal human failings — pride and anger. The relentless chain of events begins with Sedna turning away from human values by refusing to marry. She refuses to accept the normal pleasures and hardships of life, the ceaseless struggle against adversity that defines what it is to be human. Sedna's pride and her father's anger lead them to violate essential rules of behaviour. The result is an eternal separation from humankind.

Without any explanation, both accounts agree that the bird husband was a northern fulmar, a *kakoodlak* or "bird of the storm." These are the haughty white birds that nest in great numbers near the tops of high cliffs overlooking the sea. Like the raven, the fulmar is a carrion eater and is therefore spiritually dangerous. The flesh of these birds has a very unpleasant oily taste and smell. Despite this, they were hunted and eaten in the early spring for a reason explained by Peter Freuchen. "The fulmars are the first birds to appear in the spring, long before the ice breaks up. Although the flavour of their flesh is bad, the hunters go after them. After a season of nothing but walrus and bear meat, any change is for the better." The fulmar was metaphorically a visitor who seemed superficially attractive after the hardships of winter, at least in comparison with the usual fare. "Their feathers shall clothe you; your lamp shall always be filled with oil, your pot with meat." After the cold, darkness and privations of winter, the fulmar represented the promise of effortless warmth, light and abundant food.

There is a second metaphorical significance of the northern fulmar as Sedna's choice of mate. In the strongest winds, the bird of the storm is a skilful flyer. With almost rigid wings extended full length, it navigates easily with and against the wind, flying long distances with little effort. Only in calm weather does the fulmar fly with some difficulty, moving slowly with laboured wing beats just above the surface of the sea. Symbolically, the kakoodlak represented a mastery of Sila, the spirit of the storm, and the incomprehensible forces of nature. In the Sedna myth, the image of the fulmar was a visualization of a material and a spiritual freedom that the Inuit could never attain except in their imaginations.

The two versions of the legend recorded by Rasmussen and Boas are enigmatically brief and both omit many details that appear in other accounts. In her struggle beside the boat, Sedna is often described as losing an eye by being struck with an oar. More graphically, some stories have her father piercing her eye with a knife and thus killing her. In the earliest account, recorded by George Lyon, the name of the father is Anautalik, "the man with a knife." As a result of her savage treatment by her father, she lives in fear of knives, especially the shaman's knife that hangs from his amulet belt. According to some versions, her habitation at the bottom of the ocean is an ordinary igloo except that it is open at the top to enable her to watch over the Inuit. Her home is guarded by a stone wall to keep out intruders.

In all its versions, the story of the young girl was part of the common heritage of the Inuit. The Netsilik woman Nalungiark at first denied to Rasmussen that she had any special knowledge of the spirit world. "I am just an ordinary woman, knowing nothing from myself. I have never been ill and seldom dream. So I have never seen visions. . . . But what you have asked me about is something that is known to every child, every child that has been hushed to sleep with a story by its mother." Then she began her story of the mistreated orphan girl.

> I have already told you that once upon a time people believed that children could grow out of the ground just as flowers grow. Everything came from the ground; the caribou too. Everything came from the ground, and people themselves lived

71. Sarah Anirniq Kalingo   Ivujivik 1978   *Sedna and Rock*
The Big Woman lives at the bottom of the sea. Her home is protected from visitors by many large rocks. To visit her, the angakoqs must find their way through these boulders.

72. Norman Annanack Kangiqsualujjuaq 1984
Caribou Legend
In the earliest times, the animals changed their shapes without
any reason. The walrus had antlers and the caribou had tusks.
When this proved to be impractical, they agreed to exchange and
the animals assumed their present forms.

73. Novoalia Alariaq Cape Dorset 1990 *Sea Spirit*
A creature of the sea reveals its human face to speak to us.

on the ground at the time there were no animals to hunt. And they knew nothing
of all the strict taboo that we have to observe now. For no dangers threatened
them; but on the other hand no pleasures awaited them after a long day's toil.
Then it happened that a little orphan girl was thrown out into the sea when some
people were putting into a fjord in kayaks tied together. . . . Nobody cared about
the orphan girl and so she was pushed into the sea when she was trying to get
unobserved onto the kayak-raft with the others. But their wickedness turned her
into a great spirit, the greatest of all spirits we fear up here. She became Nuliajuk
and made the animals that we hunt. It was thus she took revenge, for now everything comes from her—everything that people love or fear—food and clothes,
hunger and bad hunting, abundance or lack of caribou, seals, meat and blubber.
And for her sake people had afterwards to think out all the taboo that makes it
hard to live.

Nalungiark's telling of the myth of Nuliajuk explains how their life became "one
continuous fight for food and clothing and a struggle against bad hunting and
snowstorms and sickness." With characteristic optimism, however, Nalungiark
argues that it was the creation of these dangers that gave rise to the pleasures of
life.

Only the powerful angakoqs had the ability to communicate directly with
Sedna. To reach her home, the shaman in a trance must travel to the bottom of
the sea, first crossing a narrow bridge over an abyss, then threading his way
through a dangerous field of moving boulders and passing her dog husband
guarding the entrance. This hazardous journey must be undertaken in order to
placate her wrath. When her anger was unappeased, Sedna would cause terrible
endless storms or she would cause starvation by keeping her children the sea animals with her at the bottom of the sea. Rasmussen describes the journey of a

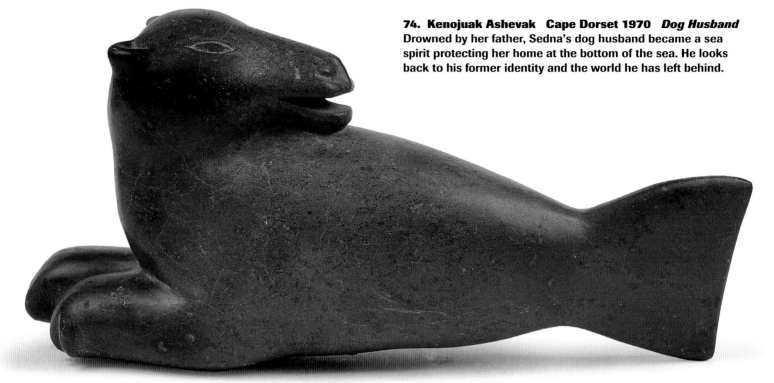

74. Kenojuak Ashevak   Cape Dorset 1970   *Dog Husband*
Drowned by her father, Sedna's dog husband became a sea
spirit protecting her home at the bottom of the sea. He looks
back to his former identity and the world he has left behind.

shaman to visit the Mistress of the Sea. Entering a trance produced by the rhythmic beat of the caribou skin drum, the angakoq invokes his helping spirits and
calls, "The way is made ready for me, the way is opening before me." When the
helping spirits arrive, the earth opens beneath the angakoq and those present cry
out together, "Let the way be open, let there be way for him!" They then hear a
voice from under the ground (the angakoq's voice) that seems to move farther
away until it is heard no longer.

During the shaman's journey, those who remain behind are in a state of
uncertainty and fearful anticipation. They sing spirit songs until the spirit of the
angakoq returns to his body.

> We stretch forth our hands
> To lift thee up.
> We are without food,
> Without fruits of our hunting,
> Come up then from below,
> From the hollow place
> Force a way through.
> We are without food,
> And here we lie down.
> We stretch forth our hands
> To lift thee up.

Fearing that they will see the spirits, the people keep their eyes tightly closed
throughout the ritual. Parents' hands firmly cover the eyes of small children.

When he reaches the house of Sedna, the angakoq breaks down the wall
that surrounds it and, showing no fear, throws aside the big dog guarding the
entrance. Calling out "I am flesh and blood," he enters to discover Sedna seated
with her back to the lamp and to the many animals gathered around her. As a

sign of her anger, her long hair is loose and dishevelled, falling over her face. Whenever a blizzard is raging, her hair streams above and behind her. Some believe that the evils of mankind drift down as lice that collect in her hair to torment her. Without fingers, she is unable to remove the lice herself. Boldly seizing hold of her, the angakoq begins to groom her hair, knowing her former pride in her appearance. As he ties her hair into a beautiful long braid, he tells her, "Those above can no longer help the seal up out of the sea." She replies, "It is your own sins and ill doing that bar the way." By means of magic words and songs that put her into a trance, the angakoq compels Sedna to give her offspring to the people above. Persuaded by the angakoq, her anger is gradually appeased and she allows the animals to return to the sea. She promises that if the people will observe her laws she will send them plenty of food and good health. The shaman then returns to the surface of the earth passing once more through the many obstacles to rejoin the living. All are eager to confess the violations of the rules and taboos that they have committed.

Despite the universal fear of Sedna's great power, there is a tone of defiance in the shaman's dangerous journey. It was a ritual performance that had as its purpose social healing. At the times of greatest need, it encouraged and strengthened community identification and solidarity. This purpose is also seen

75. Latcholassie Akesuk   Cape Dorset 1978   *Sedna with Braids*
The great sea spirit is shown with braided hair as a sign that she is at peace with the world.

in the one annual event, the Sedna festival, which brought the community together in late autumn before the family groups dispersed to their winter hunting grounds. The celebration occurred when the feverish activities of autumn had been completed. As the days became shorter, new winter clothing had been made, caches of fish and caribou meat had been accumulated, and all other preparations for the coming of winter had been accomplished. However carefully they prepared and planned, the Inuit faced the darkness and extreme cold of winter as their greatest challenge. The people of the coastal regions were dependent for survival on the success of the seal hunt on the sea ice. It was a time when the contest with Sedna and the spirit world assumed a life and death intensity. The Sedna festival reenacted this struggle in a symbolic form.

The central event of the celebration was an elaborate ritual performance led by the angakoq and several helpers. He would chant a special magic song with the onlookers accompanying him in a chorus.

> Great woman down there
> Will she, I wonder, feel a desire to move?
> Great woman down there
> Will she, I wonder, feel a desire to move?
> Will she, I wonder, feel a desire to move?
> Come out, you, down there,
> Come out, you, down there!
> Those who live above you, it is said,
> Call you
> To see you, savage and snappish,
> Come out, you, down there.

This monotonous, solemn song would lure Sedna to rise up from the depths of the sea to a breathing hole prepared in the floor of the igloo. Then with all his force the angakoq would suddenly harpoon the great spirit and a frantic tug-of-war would ensue. At the point of exhaustion, Sedna would escape and flee to her home at the bottom of the ocean. Once again she had been rejected by humankind. She took with her a new respect for the powers of the angakoq. Franz Boas gives a vivid description of one performance of this important ritual, which symbolized a defiance of the forces of nature.

> The hardest task, that of driving away Sedna, is reserved for the most powerful angakoq. A rope is coiled on the floor of a large hut in such a manner as to leave a small opening at the top, which represents the breathing hole of a seal. Two angakut stand by the side of it, one of them holding the seal spear in his left hand, as if he were waiting at the seal hole in the winter, the other holding the harpoon line. Another angakoq, whose office it is to lure Sedna up with a magic song, sits at the back of the hut. At last she comes up through the hard rocks and the wizard hears her heavy breathing; now she emerges from the ground and meets the angakoq waiting at the hole. She is harpooned and sinks away in angry haste, drawing after her the harpoon, to which the two men hold with all their strength. Only by a desperate effort does she tear herself away from it and return to her dwelling in Adlivun. Nothing is left with the two men but the blood sprinkled harpoon, which they proudly show to the Inuit.

76. Willie Fleming Kuujjuaraapik 1978 *Calling up Sedna*
"Those who live above you, it is said, call you." Assisted by his helping bear spirit, the angakoq's song lures Sedna to rise up from her home. She can be heard thrashing angrily about just below the floor of the igloo built on the winter ice.

This violent ritual contest also symbolized the seal hunt that was soon to begin on the sea ice directly above the domain of the powerful spirit. In calling up Sedna, the angakoq assumed the role of the hunters who would soon be calling up seals from the depths of the sea by means of magic words and songs. At a profound imaginative level, the contest between the angakoq and the spirit world reenacted the myth of Sedna. Eternally, she attempts to return to the human world, and the girl who would not marry is forever rejected by that world.

> Sedna and the other evil spirits are at last driven away, and on the following day a great festival for young and old is celebrated in honour of the event. But they must still be careful, for the wounded Sedna is greatly enraged and will seize any one whom she can find out of his hut. . . .

Sedna experiences an eternal exile for her denial of the human world. Despite all entreaties, she had chosen to live in a world of dreams and imagination, and there she must remain for all time.

There was great relief in the community at the outcome of the struggle with Sedna. The celebration that followed lasted several days during which the Inuit abandoned themselves to a period of carefree enjoyment with few restraints. All the celebrants attached to their hoods a piece of skin from the animal used by their mothers to clean them on the day they were born. By doing this, they believed that they were "made new." One game described by Boas was a symbolic contest between summer and winter. It was a tug-of-war between the ptarmigans, those who were born in winter, and the ducks, the children of summer. "If the ptarmigans give way the summer has won the game and fine weather may be expected through the winter." The naming ceremony that followed reaffirmed their human identity after their dangerous confrontation with the spirit world.

The contest of the seasons having been decided, the women bring out of a hut a large kettle of water and each person takes his drinking cup. They all stand as near the kettle as possible, while the oldest man among them steps out first. He dips a cup of water from the vessel, sprinkles a few drops on the ground, turns his face toward the home of his youth, and tells his name and the place of his birth. He is followed by an aged woman, who announces her name and home, and then all the others do the same, down to the young children, who are represented by their mothers. Only the parents of children born during the last year are forbidden to partake in this ceremony. As the words of the old are listened to respectfully, so those of the distinguished hunters are received with demonstrative applause and

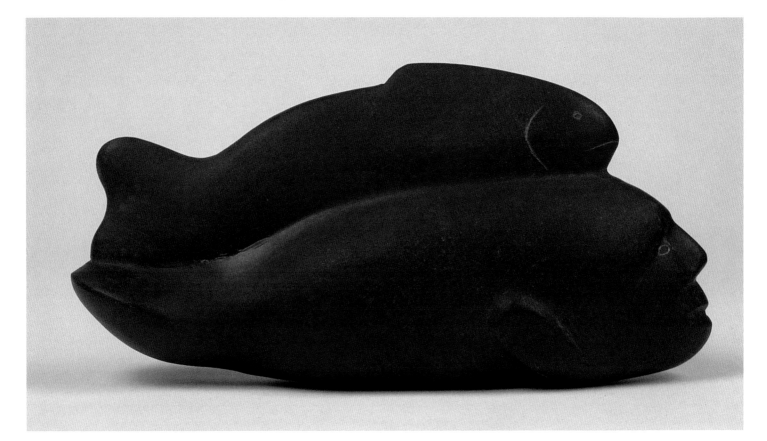

77. Barnabus Arnasungaaq Baker Lake 1991 *Shaman and Fish*
Showing his mastery of the sea creatures, the angakoq travels to visit the young girl who lives at the bottom of the sea.

those of the others with varying degrees of attention, in some cases even with joking and raillery.

When they tell their names and places of birth, they make two wishes; "They wish for calm weather and that the souls in their bodies may be calm, like the weather, for then they will be healthy and have long life."

The Sedna festival was a necessary outlet for the fears and anxieties of the Inuit when they were about to meet their greatest challenge. It allowed them to express their defiance of the spirit world and of the onset of winter. At least for a brief time it gave them an imagined control over the uncertainties of life. It brought them together in a celebration of their greatest achievement—survival as a human community in a hostile environment. The story of the young girl organized all of their experiences. Through the rituals of the Sedna myth, the Inuit were able to see their struggle to be "the people" as a spiritual confrontation with the forces of nature.

4. Raven, Can You Tell Us the Story?

COUNTLESS STORIES told and retold over the centuries in the Inuit world expressed the customs and values believed to be essential for personal and community survival. The narrative tradition continues to have a strong hold on the Inuit imagination and has become a source of creative inspiration for the modern art forms. A small sculpture (only ten centimetres high) by Daniel Angiju of Akulivik, Quebec, illustrates the story of an old woman and a bear, a tale that is familiar across a wide area of the central arctic. The following account was written by Angiju to explain his carving.

> A long time ago, the Inuit vowed to leave their relatives behind when they got old. So one day long ago, a man with his wife and children and an old woman left on a trip by dogteam. After travelling for a very long time, they became extremely hungry and they left the old woman behind. They had no choice; if they had not been threatened by starvation they would never have left her.
>
> The old woman had been alone for almost a day when she was set upon by a bear that had been following the tracks of the dog sled. As she had been walking with a cane, she placed one of her mitts on the tip of her cane and she choked the bear with it.
>
> When she had eaten enough, she followed the sled tracks herself. When she finally found her starving kin, she said to them, "Go get the bear. I left it back there, just follow the sled tracks." And so her son went by the sled to get the bear. And thus were these people saved from starvation by the bear that the old woman killed with her mitt.

This popular story demonstrates in a vivid way cultural values that are important in the struggle for survival. At times of great hardship, terrible choices must be made but, until the end, there is always hope. Whether they are orphans, the blind, the injured or the old, the weak must be protected if at all possible. They should not be abandoned since, as the story reminds us, their fortunes may change. Despite all appearances, they may still be able to contribute to the survival of the community.

Following the conventions of Inuit storytelling, Daniel Angiju relates this story as if it had really happened, although he writes that it was a long time ago. Archibald Fleming retold a very similar story that he believed had happened in recent times. Writing in the 1910s, he was convinced of the story's truthfulness since he had heard it on the authority of the James Bay district manager of the Hudson's Bay Company. This confusion about the veracity of Inuit narratives was shared by many others and reflects the problem of comprehending a different world view. Katherine Scherman was a visitor to the region of Pond Inlet and Arctic Bay in northern Baffin Island in the 1950s. She attempted to analyze the thought processes of her hunter guide Idlouk.

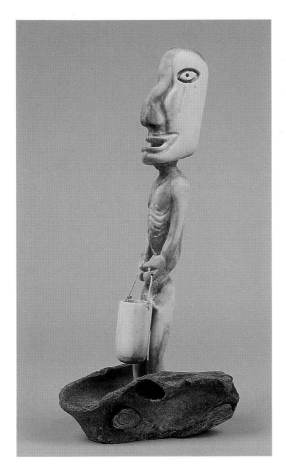

78. Daniel Kanayuk Pond Inlet 1989 *Starving Man*
"We remember the terrors of starvation. We learned how to live without food for a long time but we needed water to survive."

79. Daniel Quma Angiju Povungnituk 1978
Old Woman and Bear
The old woman had been alone for almost a day when she was set upon by a bear that had been following the tracks of the dog sled. As she had been walking with a cane, she placed one of her mitts on the tip of her cane and she choked the bear with it.

80. Anonymous Gjoa Haven 1970 *Skeletal Caribou*
The skeleton is an image of death. It is also an image of the possessing spirit, the inua of the caribou, that will lead to rebirth and renewal.

Still with all his wide and accurate knowledge of the ways of the arctic and the creatures which lived in it, our hunter could pass in an instant from fact to fantasy. Truth meant little to him and it would never occur to him (or to any other Eskimo) to say "I don't know." Whether his statement was based on careful observation or a tale told by a grandmother or a story in the bible, it was given with equal definiteness. Magic and legend had been part of his childhood, in the days when every cloud, insect, flower and animal had a spirit.

A few years earlier, the photographer and writer Doug Wilkinson lived for more than a year with the same Idlouk and his family. Wilkinson participated in hunting and experienced the rhythms of Inuit life over a full year. He was given the name Kingmik or "Dog" by his adoptive family. This was a witty play on his first name and a subtle reference to the Sedna myth. Wilkinson observed the importance of storytelling in their activities. He describes the custom, when waiting for a storm to pass or when visiting other hunting camps, of exchanging stories relating to simple incidents that occurred during hunting and travelling. "The tales are usually short and automatically told, but the Eskimos remember them. They bring quiet humour where humour could very easily not exist." During his time in the north, Wilkinson came to feel the severe limitations of the life of his adoptive family. He grew tired of the endless "talk of the hunt, of the weather, of the dogs, of the condition of the surface of the sea."

Theirs was the physical world of yesterday and today, a world they could see and feel with eye and hand. Their emotions were intense and narrow for they lived largely within themselves; fear of the unknown burned strong in their breasts. They avoided the new and the unknown and stayed close to the world they knew, a world almost untouched by beauty. No Eskimo I have met has ever been moved by the delicate curve of wind-sculptured snow, by the fragile beauty of crystals of water-washed sea ice, by the music of the wind on the sea, by the sight of a magnificent sunset in a sky of glacial blue. Even their ivory and soapstone carvings reflect their preoccupation with the world of physical things.

81. Paniluk Qamanirq   Arctic Bay 1974   *Inua*
Manasie Akpaliapik explained that his grandmother Paniloo believed that everything in nature had a spirit. When they gave names to the natural landmarks in their environment, they tried to see or imagine the inua of the rocks, mountains and lakes.

Both observers seem to have missed essential aspects of the Inuit imagination. In the narrative tradition, psychological and spiritual truth are more important than the narrow concept of reality advocated by Scherman. The mythological framework accepted by Idlouk made connections between aspects of reality that outsiders would characterize as fantasy. The pragmatic emphasis on the physical world that Wilkinson observed was undoubtedly present. In a

82. James Ungalaq   Igloolik 1991   *Healing*
The angakoq opposes the powers causing sickness with his physical and spiritual strength. He kneels over the patient to force the evil spirit to flee.

83. Ovilu Tunnilie   Cape Dorset c.1970   *Breath*
Baring his chest to show his humanity in the confrontation with the spirit world, the angakoq attempts to expel evil spirits and to join his breath to the Great Spirit of the Air. The artist expresses the mental and physical strain of the shamanic performances.

difficult environment, it could not be otherwise. At the same time, there was a spiritual context to all Inuit activities that he was not equipped to see. Idlouk would have found it very difficult to explain this spiritual background to his activities since it was self-evident in his mental picture of the world. Fundamentally, Idlouk did not see himself as separated from the nature in which he lived and breathed. Wilkinson's last comments are impossible to reconcile with the subsequent development of Inuit art. Unfortunately, we have no record of Idlouk's views of the limitations of these travellers, with the possible exception of one comment that he made about Kingmik, "Sometimes he even thinks a bit like an Eskimo."

The logic of Inuit thought was expressed not in propositions but in stories, metaphors and images. It was based more on observing correlations of events and behaviours than on extended logical deductions and either–or classifications. At the same time, there was in the traditional life a high value placed on practical intellectual activity. This is indicated by the use of the word *isuma* for "thought" or "wisdom," which derives from the root *isu* meaning "the end" or

84. David Ruben Piqtoukun   Paulatuk, Toronto 1990

85. Novoalia Alariaq   Cape Dorset 1990

86. Tujeatsiak   Repulse Bay c. 1968

87. Mark Tungilik   Repulse Bay c. 1970

88. Jimmy Nookiguak   Broughton Island c. 1980

89. Isa Aupalukta   Inukjuak c. 1975

In shamanic cultures, birds are seen as representations of the shaman's flight to another world to mediate between humankind and the mysterious forces of nature. Birds in flight represent the angakoq's soul, a messenger from the spirit domain, and the power of Sila. Angakoqs are closely identified with water birds (fulmars, loons, geese), expressing a mastery of earth, sea and sky. Bird symbolism is not restricted to shamanism but is common to all religions.

"the ultimate" in the sense of purpose. It was believed that isuma was acquired at the age of twelve or thirteen, after which children were expected to behave responsibly. The word for leader is *isumatok*, which means "the one who takes thought." A leader was respected primarily for the ability to think and the phrase *isumatuujuk*, "he is well endowed with thought," was a great compliment. A powerful shaman was *silatuujuk*, "well endowed with spirit or life force." Between the isumatok and the angakoq in an Inuit community, there was a healthy balance of pragmatic and spiritual wisdom. Both qualities could be combined in the same person, although this was unusual since the two roles required different personalities. As Peter Freuchen points out, "a great hunter and outstanding provider is such because he is quiet and sober, while an angakoq most often is a less successful hunter, a man who suffers under the monotony of daily routine, and who is only called upon in the hour of need."

During the time he lived with the Caribou Eskimo, Kaj Birket-Smith observed that there was no faulting Inuit powers of perception in situations that their experiences had equipped them to understand. "As soon as they catch sight of a caribou they visualize the hundred details of the forms of the landscape, wind and weather, and vegetation on which the successful outcome of the chase depends. Travelling in their own country they almost unconsciously absorb innumerable impressions which serve to guide them. . . . On the other hand, I have seen an intelligent Greenlander stand quite lost in a city right beside the hotel we lived in. He had not yet become accustomed to discriminate amid city architecture, illuminated shop windows, and electric signs in the same manner as we do." Both Scherman and Wilkinson came to appreciate the skill and creativity that Idlouk demonstrated in hunting. He was given the name "unborn seal" at birth so that he would become a great hunter of seals. Scherman recorded a fragmentary story about a legendary hunter with the same name.

> Once, a long time ago, a man decided he would live in the bodies of all the animals in turn to see which he liked best. He tried caribou, wolf, fox, jaeger, weasel and seal. When he came home he said that it was best being a seal. He was named Idlouk and he became the greatest seal hunter of his people.

Scherman concluded that the Idlouk she knew must have lived in a seal at some time. He always had an uncanny knowledge of what they would do next.

A more recent observer of life in the north has written a very human memoir describing a typical year in the 1970s in the Igloolik and Repulse Bay areas. Writing under the pen name Georgia, she tells a revealing story of a visitor to Rankin Inlet, a middle-aged anthropology summer researcher. Georgia was not very sympathetic when she found this anthropologist admonishing a four-year-old boy not to throw rocks at the birds. He did not recognize that the young child was playing at being a hunter and he was not able to believe that the child's parents would praise their son if he managed to hit his target. From an early age, Inuit children were encouraged to contribute to the food supplies of their families. Clearly, the visitor had some shortcomings as an anthropologist. This pointed anecdote illustrates the problem of interpreting and controlling behaviour from the perspectives of a different culture. One time, Duncan Pryde and the hunter Palvik observed the approach of a countless herd of caribou. As the

90. Barnabus Arnasungaaq
Baker Lake 1990 *Muskox Spirit*
The hunters feared to offend the spirits of the
animals they hunted.

91. Mona Kohoktak Tigitok   Coppermine 1981
Bear Shaman
Fishing was often left to women and children. The *ulu* (woman's
knife) and mitten suggest that a woman has called on a bear
spirit to help her in fishing.

92. Johnny Aculiak   Inukjuak 1978 *Hunting Seals*
A great hunter enters the soul of the seal to hunt seals at their
breathing holes.

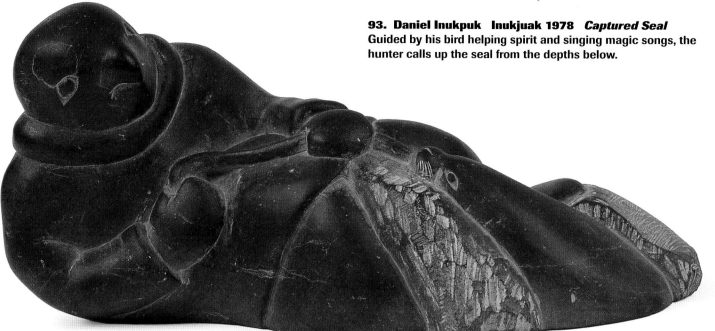

93. Daniel Inukpuk Inukjuak 1978 *Captured Seal*
Guided by his bird helping spirit and singing magic songs, the hunter calls up the seal from the depths below.

94. Novoalia Alariaq Cape Dorset 1990 *Trance*
The trance state of the soul journey.

95. Novoalia Alariaq Cape Dorset 1990 *Vision*
The unseeing eyes of the shamanic vision.

96. Nick Sikkuark   Pelly Bay 1988   *Bolo Hunter*
Bolos were thrown at the low-flying shore birds that nested in
great numbers in the early summer. The hunter has entered the
spirit of the bird.

97. Josiah Nuilaalik   Baker Lake 1991   *Caribou Shaman*
An angakoq with realistic caribou antlers and emerging wings,
common symbols in shamanic cultures. The ivory inset face
shows the separation of spirit and body.

animals came nearer, Pryde cried out, "What an amazing sight!" Palvik replied, "*Niqiraaluit*! What a lot of food!" In their different ways, both exclamations drew attention to the spiritual, religious quality of the experience. The middle-aged anthropologist and the four-year-old boy in Rankin Inlet may not have understood each other, but they were both defending human values.

Some stories document in a realistic way events of great importance to the community. The title of a 1977 Davidialuk print "Story of Aukautik Attacking a Woman" can be seen as a description of the sculpture created at about the same time by Aisa Tuluga of Povungnituk. On the base of his carving of the murder scene he wrote the following text in syllabics. His account has the immediacy and confusion of an eyewitness report.

> Aukautik was killing the people. The lady got killed trying to get into the igloo. The man hiding behind the *kamotik* [sled] is being fired at by Aukautik. He is trying to find his bullets from his *kamotik* box. He is holding his knife. His name is Audlaluk. The police saw the blood as soon as they arrived at the village. They were pulling their kamotiks toward the village. The wife tried to enter the igloo. As soon as she got close, she was killed.

To interpret this very direct story, we must be aware of the rigid rules of hospitality in Inuit life that Aukautik was breaking so violently. One incident among the Copper Eskimo recorded by Rasmussen illustrated the extent to which a man's home was considered a sanctuary. When Heq had his wife stolen from him, he tried in vain to lure the abductor out of his tent. Heq could not bring himself to

98. Aisa Amaruali Tuluga   Povungnituk 1978 *Murder Scene*
"Aukatik was killing the people." A documentary sculpture describing a memorable incident.

99. Passa Saviardjuk Kavavou   Ivujivik 1978
My Children
"These are my children. They are starving to death.
We are trying to walk inland...With my husband lost or
drowned or eaten by a polar bear...."

attack a man in his own home whatever the provocation. It may be significant that Aisa Tuluga's documentary sculpture draws attention to the rifle as the key factor in disrupting traditional values. Audlaluk has only his knife with which to defend himself.

A sculpture by Passa Kavavou of Ivujivik, Quebec, records some vivid and painful personal memories, experiences that all Inuit families remember.

These are my children. They are starving to death. We are trying to walk inland. My husband went hunting one morning. He was supposed to come back that night, but he hasn't returned. We don't know what happened to him. My children will starve to death. That's why we have started to walk. It's a good thing I carried some blankets. During the night we need them. Even with them, sometimes the children wake up because there aren't enough and they get too cold. Sometimes we keep walking because they feel better walking than sleeping. With my husband lost, or drowned or eaten by a polar bear, we are trying to reach the place where we all were last year, but we don't know exactly which direction to go. Also, what will I do without my husband? We have even lost our dogs. Please, my husband, come back! Please come back! Ai ya ya! Ai ya ya!

In her telling of this deeply felt story, Kavavou comes very close to composing a traditional song.

100. Levi Qumaluk   Povungnituk c. 1975   *Giant*
"For all their bigness and strength, the Tunit were a
stupid, slow-going race (according to the Eskimo
version), and fell an easy prey to the Eskimo, who used
to stalk them and hunt them down like game.... They
were so strong that one of them could hold a walrus as
easily as an Eskimo a seal.... They did not hunt deer
like the Eskimo, but erected long lines of stone 'men'
in a valley through which the deer passed. The deer
would pass between the lines of stones, and the
hunters behind them would lance them." (Hawkes, 143)

101, 102. Johnny Kakutuk   Akulivik 1978   *Someone Is Telling a Story*
(101) This story is about a man who could change to any kind of animal. The change first
took place when he was eaten by a bear. After a while he turned into a bear. Whenever
he was eaten, he would turn into the animal that ate him.
(102) Before the man turned into a bear, he liked to eat human flesh. The man-bear
thinks he is still a human so he continues his cannibalism. The carving shows a fresh kill.
The man-bear is lifting a head. His knapsack is full of the man's flesh. He is also using the
dead man's parka.

103. Osuitok Ipeelee   Cape Dorset 1965   *Embryonic Bird*
The bird embryo expresses the idea that the angakoq and the
hunter enter totally into the spirit of the bird, even into the body
of the bird.

104. Joseph Suqslak   Gjoa Haven 1992   *Bear Hunter*
When stalking seals near their breathing holes, a hunter must
imitate the infinite patience of the animal without a shadow. He
must enter the spirit of the polar bear.

The Inuit's use of language could be precise and evocative when describing the world they knew, but fell short when used to convey the world outside. Uisaakassak was a Polar Eskimo who spent one year in the New York area in 1897-98 at the invitation of Franz Boas, then the director of the American Museum of Natural History. When he returned to the north, he attempted to describe the marvels he had seen "among the man-made mountains," but he was handicapped by the lack of an appropriate vocabulary. Out of necessity, he used some familiar images to describe his experiences.

> The ships sailed in and out there, like eiders on the brooding cliffs when their young begin to swim. There weren't many free drops of water in the harbour itself; it was filled with ships. You'd risk your life if you tried to go out there in a kayak, you'd simply not be noticed, and you'd be run down unmercifully. People lived up in the air like auks on a bird cliff. The houses are as big as icebergs on a glacial bank, and they stretch inland as far as you can see, like a steep chain of mountains with innumerable canyons that serve as roads.
>
> And the people. Yes, there are so many of them that when smoke rises from the chimneys and the women are about to make breakfast, clouds fill the sky and the sun is eclipsed.
>
> The streetcars, big as houses, with masses of glass windows as transparent as freshwater ice, raced on without dogs to haul them, without smoke, and full of smiling people who had no fear of their fate. And all this just because a man pulled on a cord.
>
> He, Uisaakassak, had stood and talked to [Robert] Peary, who was visiting another village. Without shouting at one another, they had talked together through a funnel, along a cord.

At this point, he was interrupted by old Soqqaq, the angakoq, who told him, "Uisaakassak! It appears that you have been far away and no longer know the truth. Go to the women with your lies!" Soqqaq had visited the spirit world many times and had never seen anything so unusual. Others objected that it would be impossible to find enough wood to make so many ships. The breaking point occurred when he said that his voice had been carried through a tiny thread to speak without shouting to the American arctic explorer Robert Peary, who at the time was several sleeps distant. For the rest of his life, Uisaakassak was called "The Big Liar." There is a character in Greenland folklore with this unfortunate nickname. In 1907, when Rasmussen attempted to defend him, he was told, "Yes, Uisaakassak was a great hunter, he had the best dogs, and was awfully good company; but you could never believe what he told you, for he was incorrigible and full of lies." By the summer of 1910, his boastfulness and erratic behaviour had become intolerable to many of the Polar Eskimos. He was killed during a narwhal hunt by Sigluk and Uutaaq, two community leaders who had accompanied Peary one year before on his final journey to the North Pole. They needed wives and the unbearable Uisaakassak happened to have two.

The reception that Uisaakassak's story encountered echoed the experience of John Ross who, as captain of the *Isabella*, was a leader of the British Navy expedition that reached the lands of the Polar Eskimo in 1818. He gave the first descriptions of this remote people.

They exist in a corner of the world by far the most secluded which has yet been discovered, and have no knowledge of any thing but what originates, or is found in their own country; nor have they any tradition how they came to this spot, or from whence they came; having, until the moment of our arrival, believed themselves to be the only inhabitants of the universe, and that all the rest of the world was a mass of ice.

The natives were astonished by the ships of the expedition, believing them to be living creatures with great wings. They asked the ships directly, "Who are you? What are you? Where do you come from? The sun or the moon? Do you give us light by night or by day?" They appealed to the sailors, "Don't destroy us! We are alive, very much alive!", recalling words used by the angakoqs in the journeys to the spirit world. When his expedition returned to England, the account that Ross gave of these people was very harshly criticized by John Barrow, the Admiralty Secretary responsible for Britain's arctic exploration. Barrow maintained that Ross could not have seen what he claimed and that, in all probability, he had never left his ship.

There were complex motivations for Soqqaq's rejection of Uisaakassak's descriptions of the outside world. True to his name, "The Whalebone," which conveyed hardness and strength, Soqqaq was a man who expressed himself in the most direct way. He said that the greatest happiness of his life was to run across fresh bear tracks and be ahead of the other sledges. When Rasmussen asked him to describe his adventures when hunting polar bears, he replied with his usual bluntness.

> One must not talk about bear-hunting; if one's thoughts turn upon bears, then drive out and kill some. But sit inside and prate upon them? No, leave that to old women; they are never backward when it is a case of chattering. But we men, we drive out one day with our dogs, and if we see a bear, it is not long before its meat is in our cooking pot. I have nothing more to say!

But there is a deeper reason for his objections to Uisaakassak's fables. In 1864, a small group of Inuit had migrated from Baffin Island to the lands of the Polar Eskimo, bringing with them different customs and a superior hunting technology. Peter Freuchen recorded the reactions of Soqqaq to the arrival of these new people. "He had once been the greatest hunter and angakoq in the tribe, and had never ceased to resent the invasion of natives from Admiralty Bay who had brought with them the kayak and the bow and arrow, and had so coloured the lives of the people who had been there before them. Soqqaq never adopted the new ways, and consequently the newcomers had usurped a great deal of his glory." Soqqaq's son Tatterat developed a gradual paralysis that was attributed to the evil powers of Kritlaq, the visiting angakoq. In Uisaakassak's account of the wonders of the white man's world, Soqqaq must have seen the danger of a repetition of his experiences more than three decades before.

By refusing to talk about his exploits in hunting bears, Soqqaq was following Inuit values that discouraged all self-praise and boastfulness. In the 1950s, the Dutch ethnologist Geert van den Steenhoven recorded the ironic song of a Caribou Eskimo hunter that expressed these values.

> It is a time of hunger,
> But I don't feel like hunting,
> I don't care for the advice of the old people,
> I only care for dreaming, wishing, nothing else,
> I only care for gossip;
> I am fond of young caribou,
> The age they start getting their antlers;
> Nobody is like me,
> I am too lazy, simply too lazy,
> I just can't bring myself to go and get some meat.

Only a very great hunter would dare to sing a song like this.

There are some Inuit stories that have an almost scientific purpose, observing and attempting to explain aspects of the natural world in terms more believable than Uisaakassak's inventions. An interesting example is the story of the Great Flood collected by Franz Boas, a tale that is believed to predate the introduction of Christianity.

> A long time ago the ocean suddenly began to rise, until it covered the whole land. The water even rose to the top of the mountains and the ice drifted over them. When the flood had subsided the ice stranded and ever since forms an ice cap on the top of the mountains. Many shellfish, fish, seals and whales were left high and dry and their shells and bones may be seen to this day. A great number of Inuit died during this period, but many others, who had taken to their kayaks when the water commenced to rise, were saved.

When climbing the inland mountains near Pond Inlet, Katherine Scherman found many sea shells and fossilized whale bones at heights far above sea level. She asked Idlouk where the bones had come from. Without hesitating, he answered "The Bible. Genesis Seven." Idlouk was seeking new explanations for the phenomena of nature from the one book that he owned. He admitted to Wilkinson that he did not find easy to understand the contents of this well-worn volume printed in syllabic characters. "I must be very dense. I read what it says here, I know what I read, yet how often I cannot understand it. But no matter, I believe, and that is what is important."

The following legend of the origin of the winds and rain was recorded among the Labrador Eskimo by the anthropologist E. W. Hawkes in the early years of this century. It resembles a supernatural weather report.

> There is a giant spirit who lives in the north. When he blows his breath, violent snowstorms occur. Other spirits live in the east and west. They breathe soft winds and summer weather. Female spirits dwell to the south. They send the flowers and summer rain. They live up in the sky and keep the rain in big bags. When they run across the sky the water escapes. The thunder is the noise of their running across the sky.

There was a great concern in the traditional life to account for the behaviour of the winds and the origins of storms. The old angakoq Ilatsiak confessed to Diamond Jenness that he did not know what became of the winds in calm weather. He did know that they would blow hard "if the women sewed new deerskin clothes during the dark days of winter, or if in spring and summer the Eskimos lingered too long round the lakes and islands, or ate the lungs of the caribou." Ilatsiak's concern to understand the behaviour of the winds expressed in an indirect way his inability despite all his knowledge and experience to comprehend fully the behaviour of the great spirits or forces of nature.

Attempting to gain knowledge of the spirit world was always dangerous, as we learn from an old story recorded by Franz Boas, "The Woman and the Spirit of the Singing House."

Once upon a time a woman entered the singing house when it was quite dark. For a long time she had wished to see the spirit of the house, and though the Inuit had warned her of the impending danger she had insisted upon her undertaking.

She summoned the spirit, saying, "If you are in the house, come here." As she could not see him, she cried, "No spirit is here; he will not come." But the spirit, though yet invisible, said, "Here I am; there I am." Then the woman asked, "Where are your feet; where are your shins; where are your thighs; where are your hips; where are your loins?" Every time the spirit answered, "Here they are; there they are." And she asked further, "Where is your belly?" "Here it is," answered

105. Kaka Ashoona Cape Dorset 1991 *Spirit Head*
Another creature that visits in dreams.

106. Davidialuk Alasua Amittu Povungnituk c. 1965
Katyutayuuq
Katyutayuuq was heard in the dark nights of winter beating on the igloo, threatening those inside who had broken the taboos. Davidialuk sees her as a frightening bodiless spirit with breasts on the cheeks of her large head.

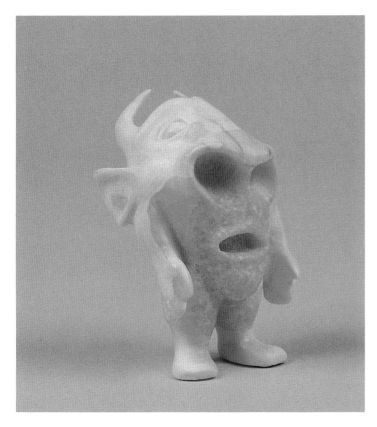

107. Novoalia Alariaq   Cape Dorset 1990   *Spirit Head*
A visualization of a tupilak, a bodiless demon seen by the
imagination.

108. Anonymous   Spence Bay c. 1970   *Tupilak*
"We wear amulets and follow many rules to protect ourselves
from evil spirits."

the spirit. "Where is your breast; where are your shoulders; where is your neck; where is your head?" "Here it is; there it is"; but in touching the head the woman all of a sudden fell dead. It had no bones and no hair.

Despite her earnest efforts, the unfortunate woman learned very little about the unseen forces. Only through the rituals of the angakoqs could the spirits be approached safely. They must be spoken to in the secret shamanic language learned after a long apprenticeship; one of the first tasks of a novice angakoq was to learn the secret terms for the parts of the body.

Beyond the many stories that were believed to have taken place however long ago, there are numerous legends that have a more tenuous historical basis. It was believed that the Inuit shared their land in the old times with other human-like beings, both dwarves and giants. The giants, identified as the Tunit, were much stronger than ordinary people, but they could be outwitted since they were not very intelligent. The dwarves were much more dangerous since they were very crafty and always did unexpected things. It is interesting to speculate that these tales of dwarves and giants reflect a dim memory of other population groups that have lived in the north. The stone houses found in ruins in many regions of the Arctic are identified by the Inuit as the work of the vanished Tunit people. Idlouk told Scherman that a people he called the Toonijuk lived in these abandoned ruins "long ago, before my grandfather was born." Rasmussen concluded, from the evidence of these archaeological sites, that the Tunit were identical with the Inuit who had settled Greenland a thousand years before. His companions from Greenland, Miteq and Anarulunguaq, seemed to feel thoroughly at home among these ruins.

Daniel Qumak of Akulivik tells the well-known story, both in his sculpture and in a written version, of the man smothered by a dwarf.

> Hunting with his dogteam, an inuk encounters a dwarf. Suddenly without any warning, the dwarf attacks the man by jumping onto him, covering his mouth and nose. Almost dying, the man falls backward to the ground. The hunter's dogs then attack the dwarf and kill him since the man, out of breath, cannot call them off. The man is saved by his dogs. He does not know why the dwarf attacked him.

This brief story has elements that are related to the central themes of Inuit narratives. The dwarf is probably a malevolent spirit sent to punish the man's transgression of the rules governing Inuit life. The taboo that the hunter had violated has been long forgotten by him but not by the offended spirit. Vengeance was inevitable although it might be delayed for a time. The hunt was a particularly dangerous time since it was a direct confrontation with the unseen forces. By cutting off the hunter's breath, the dwarf attempts to break the hunter's connection with life.

109. Daniel Quma Angiju Akulivik 1978 *Dwarf Story*

110. Aisa Amittu   Akulivik 1979 *Dwarf Story*

Hunting with his dogteam, a man encounters a dwarf. Suddenly, the dwarf attacks the man by jumping onto him and covering his mouth and nose.

An even stranger fable was told by Minnie Palliser of Inukjuak, Quebec. This is the story of the lonely woman and her worm child, a legend known as far away as Greenland.

> A woman was living with her brothers, who would not allow their sister to marry. Every human suitor was turned away by the brothers who needed her to make their clothes and prepare their food. There were no women for the brothers to marry.
>
> In her loneliness, the sister listened to the entreaties of a giant worm. She ran away from her brothers to live with the worm. For a long time, the brothers did not find where she and the worm were living but, when they found her, they killed her worm husband and they forced her to return to live with them. They did allow her worm child to live and she loved it very much.

This unusual story encodes many of the beliefs and values of Inuit life. A woman experiencing adversity would say, "If only I had a brother." By not allowing their sister to marry, the brothers acted against one of the fundamental rules of nature. Once they had broken this basic law for selfish reasons, unpredictable disastrous consequences must follow. The woman responds by breaking an even stronger taboo. Her choice of mate emphasizes the rejection of normal life since there was a traditional fear and even dread of worms. She turns away from her own kind to

111. Minnie Palliser   Inukjuak 1978
Worm Child
In her loneliness, the sister listened to the entreaties of a giant worm. She ran away from her brothers to live with the worm.

live in the animal world. This tragic theme, the loss of human identity, occurs repeatedly in Inuit narratives.

The bond of marriage was seen as a fundamental aspect of human identity and it provides the theme for very many stories. "A woman without a lamp" was an image that symbolized an unmarried woman and conveyed complete deprivation. Very frequently in contemporary carvings, a woman is represented with a *kudlik*, a soapstone lamp, to indicate that she has a husband and family. A bachelor almost always appears in Inuit stories as a ridiculous figure. This subject is treated with wry humour in the Polar Eskimo fable recorded by Rasmussen, "The Raven Who was Anxious to be Married."

> A little sparrow was grieving for her husband who had not returned. She was fond of him because he used to catch worms for her. As she sat weeping, a raven came up to her and asked, "What are you crying for?"
>
> "I am crying for my husband who has not returned. I was fond of him because he caught worms for me," said the sparrow.
>
> "Weeping is not seemly for those who can hop about on the top of the blades of grass. Marry me — me, with my lovely high forehead, broad temples, long beard and large beak. You shall sleep under my wings, and dainty dung shall be your food."
>
> "I will not marry you, just because you have a high forehead, broad temples, long beard, and large beak — and because you offer me dung for food."
>
> So the raven went his way, and went to make love to the wild geese. And he was so sick with love that he could not sleep. The wild geese were just about to fly away when he reached them.
>
> "As a silly sparrow has rejected me, I should like to marry you," said the raven to two geese.
>
> "You arrive just as we are about to fly away," said the geese.
>
> "I will come with you," said the raven.
>
> "But see, that is impossible for anyone who cannot rest on the sea. There are no icebergs that way."
>
> "Never mind! I will sail through the air." And so he took the two geese as his wives. Then the wild geese set off and the raven with them, but it was not long before he began to drop behind, he was so tired and drowsy. "Something to rest upon! Place yourselves side by side!" he cried. And his two wives placed themselves side by side on the water while their comrades went on.
>
> The raven settled himself upon their backs and fell asleep. But when his wives saw the other wild geese getting farther and farther away, they shook the raven off into the sea and flew on.
>
> "Something to rest upon!" shrieked the raven, as it fell with a great splash into the water. At last it sank to the bottom and was drowned. Afterwards it broke up into small pieces, and its soul became little "sea ravens" (black pteropods).

It is not difficult to see beyond the humour of this story of the lovesick raven to detect some serious themes. Blinded by pride and desire, the raven loses sight of his identity. The sparrow and the two geese behave very differently. This legend encouraged children (and not only children) to accept their own natures and to take their normal places in human society. The listeners were also aware of a second level of interpretation based on the raven as a metaphor for the angakoq.

The proud boast of his powers, "Never mind! I will sail through the air," is a defiance of the spirit world that must end in disaster.

A third artist from Akulivik, Makusi Anauta, relates another tale of an unusual marriage, the story of a young girl and an eagle. The roots of this story are familiar in every area of the north, but it is told in many versions. The village of Akulivik (formerly called Cape Smith) was abandoned in the 1950s at the time of a virulent tuberculosis epidemic. It became necessary to evacuate a sizable proportion of the population (about one in three) to hospitals in the south. Many never returned to their homes. Most of those who did not travel south moved to a more settled life in Povungnituk, where health and social services could be obtained. Twenty years later, several families decided to resettle in Akulivik. Their aim was to live a more traditional way of life where outside influences could be better controlled. It is a common attitude among Inuit old enough to remember the former way of life that the relatively large communities developed since 1950 are not their real homes. These are still to be found at the old hunting camps even if they are now visited only rarely or never.

Since Akulivik has been resettled by people attempting to recapture part of their authentic culture, it is not surprising that much of the art produced there has been inspired by the narrative tradition. Makusi Anauta tells his violent story in three parts, each illustrated by a dramatic sculpture.

> An eagle picked up a young girl, flew her up to a high cliff and made her his wife. The young girl was forced to stay on the cliff because she could not climb up or down. For a long time they lived together and the girl became pregnant. When the eagle asked her what kind of food she wanted to eat, the young girl would answer that she wanted a whole young caribou. The girl had a reason for asking for this meat. She planned to make an escape line from the caribou sinew, to make it long enough to go down the cliff. The eagle hunted all day so the girl had time to braid the sinews into a strong line. One day, she managed to escape from the eagle. The eagle went up to find her at her old home. He asked the people where his wife was.
>
> Seeing the eagle, a man killed him. He had a reason for killing the eagle; he wanted the eagle's wife for his own. The man married the young girl not knowing that she was already pregnant by her previous husband. The young girl used to complain to her new husband that he could not hunt as well as her dead husband, the eagle. Sometimes she was angry when he returned from hunting without any meat.
>
> The young girl dearly loved her baby from her first husband, a baby eagle. She loved her baby eagle so much that she always carried it in her *amautik* (parka hood). Even when she had another baby from her human husband, she loved her baby eagle more and she never carried the younger baby in her amautik. The husband was very angry because his wife did not look after her younger child better than the baby eagle. Because of his love for his son, he became so angry that he killed the young girl.

It is probably significant that Anauta's legend describes the abduction of a young girl from her home and the subsequent struggle to return. Even after her escape, problems continue. "The young girl used to complain to her husband

112, 113, 114. Makusi Pangutu Anauta   Akulivik 1978
Woman and Eagle
(112) "An eagle picked up a young girl, flew her up to a high cliff and made her his wife... For a long time they lived together and the girl became pregnant...."
(113) "Seeing the eagle, a man killed him. He had a reason for killing the eagle; he wanted the eagle's wife for his own...."
(114) "The young girl dearly loved her baby from her first husband, a baby eagle...."

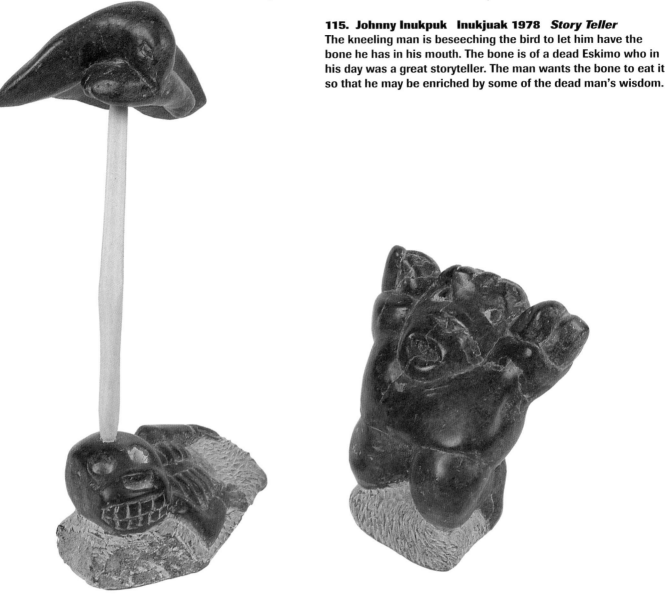

115. Johnny Inukpuk Inukjuak 1978 *Story Teller*
The kneeling man is beseeching the bird to let him have the bone he has in his mouth. The bone is of a dead Eskimo who in his day was a great storyteller. The man wants the bone to eat it so that he may be enriched by some of the dead man's wisdom.

that he could not hunt as well as her dead husband, the eagle." Metaphorically, the story centres on the attempt of the Akulivik people to achieve a workable synthesis of their former life and the new influences.

Many sculptures that relate to the narrative tradition are very difficult to analyze satisfactorily. This is the case with the sculpture of the skeleton and the raven by Johnny Inukpuk, a well-known artist from Inukjuak. The symbolism of the carving clearly relates to shamanism in many ways. When he journeys to the spirit world, the angakoq leaves his body or skeleton behind. At the moment when the angakoq's spirit takes flight, a bird (often a raven) may be seen flying over the igloo. In an interview in the early 1960s, the artist related the following puzzling story to explain a similar sculpture.

The man says: You have something in your mouth which I have not been near enough to touch.

The bird says: It is a person's thigh, because it is sweet and I like the smell of it. I like it even better when it is frozen.

The kneeling man is beseeching the bird to let him have the bone he has in his mouth. The bone is of a dead Eskimo who in his day was a great storyteller. The man wants the bone to eat it that he may be enriched with some of the dead man's wisdom.

In some areas, the angakoq was traditionally referred to as a storyteller and that may explain the reference here. The Polar Eskimo Osarqaq told Rasmussen, "when I narrate legends, it is not I who speak, it is the wisdom of our forefathers speaking through me." This is similar to the claim of the angakoqs that in their performances they became the voices of the spirits possessing them. More recently, the term storyteller has become a convenient euphemism for angakoq, useful to those who are reluctant to discuss the old beliefs.

At a very immediate level, the raven was identified as a storyteller or a source of knowledge. Ravens have an uncanny ability to mimic other birds and animals. When Polar Eskimos in northern Greenland saw one or two ravens flying in a certain directions, they would call out, "*Nanu-qapa! Nanu-qapa!*" — "Is there any bear? Is there any bear?" They believed that the ravens would answer if they were flying to see if the bears had caught something. On Baffin Island and in the Barren Lands to the west, the Inuit asked the ravens flying over if there were any caribou to be found. At another level, the image of a bird hovering above is an indication of the presence of the spirit world and it is also a representation of the angakoq's power to see far away. A spirit song recorded by Rasmussen takes this as its theme and suggests other interpretations of Inukpuk's sculpture.

> The little seamew
> Hovers above us,
> Staring and scolding.
> Its head is white.
> Its beak opens gaping,
> The little round eyes
> See far, see keenly.
> *Qutiuk, qutiuk!*
>
> The little tern
> Hovers above us,
> Staring and scolding.
> Its head is black.
> Its beak opens gaping,
> The little round eyes
> See far, see keenly.
> *Iyoq-iyoq!*
>
> The big raven
> Hovers above us,
> Staring and scolding.
> Its head is black.
> Its beak is sharp,
> As if it had teeth.
> *Qara-qara!*

A story from northern Alaska recorded by Robert Spencer also centres on the connections of the raven, the storyteller and the angakoq.

116. Eli Sallualu Qinuajua   Povungnituk c. 1965   *Shame*
"This is what happens when you have venereal disease." This sculpture was intended as the equivalent of a shaming song. In the traditional culture, individuals whose behaviour was not acceptable would be mercilessly ridiculed during a song festival.

There was a raven who flew over two people who couldn't find their son. They asked him: "Raven, can you tell us the story? You were flying over us." And the raven answered:

> What then? What then?
> What shall I tell the two of you?
> Up at the mountain,
> Between them,
> There is your son.
> We have eaten him.
> Is he the one you ask about?

And the woman answered, singing:

> I wonder what it is
> I throw at him,
> With meat, with an eye.

The raven or the angakoq's helping spirit can tell us the story, but the knowledge that it brings may not be welcome.

A second sculpture that is a challenge to analyze is the exaggerated carving by Eli Sallualu of Povungnituk, an artist best known for his intricately carved anthropomorphic spirit sculptures. The story told by Sallualu to explain this imaginative work can be related in one sentence; "This is what happens when you have venereal disease." That is the official explanation written in inuktitut

117. Osuitok Ipeelee Cape Dorset c. 1970 *Sedna and Hare*
When asked to tell the story, Osuitok remembered that the hare is faster than the fox in daylight but the fox is a better hunter in the dark. There is a story that the exhausted hare saw that the sea animals did not fear the fox. He asked for Sedna's protection.

syllabics on the sculpture, but there is believed to be a subtext to this simple narrative. One member of the community was being criticized for his habit of not joining the other men when they travelled to the hunting grounds. For reasons that were not acceptable to the hunters, he preferred to remain behind to keep company with the women. Following an old Inuit tradition, this carving was made to ridicule his behaviour. In times past, a shaming song would have been composed to achieve the same result.

A third sculpture that needs explanation is the carving of Sedna and the arctic hare by Osuitok of Cape Dorset. When asked by one of us to tell the story behind his creation, the artist said something to the effect that "the hare is faster than the fox in daylight but the fox is a better hunter in the dark." This recalls a story recorded by Peter Freuchen and others. "In the beginning, the fox asked for eternal darkness so that it could easily steal from the meat caches of the humans, while the arctic hare asked for continual light so that it could find food in the grass. As a compromise, light and darkness have ever since alternated on the earth." This may be the basic story, but evidently we are missing some important details when we attempt to relate it to Osuitok's carving. This uncertainty allows the viewers of this sculpture to participate in the oldest storytelling tradition of all. They can improvise, creating their own stories.

George Swinton relates a more recent Baffin Island story that demonstrates that the narrative tradition continues to develop within the old conventions.

> In Cape Dorset, Niviaksiak's death in 1959 is still considered a mystery. He went hunting one day with a companion, and they tracked a bear for hours. When they caught up with him, the bear suddenly turned around. Niviaksiak raised the rifle, but he did not fire; he collapsed and died. His companion ran. The next day, the dead body was still there — untouched; the nearest bear tracks were some twenty feet away. The R.C.M.P. reported "death from natural causes," but the people because of Niviaksiak's concentration on the carving of bears, sensed supernatural intervention: punishment for searching beyond man's depth.

This very visual documentary account of Niviaksiak's death is clearly on its way to becoming a legend and myth. Remarkably, the story places the new activity of carving firmly inside the framework of the old beliefs.

One story leads to another in a chain that never ends, since the proper response to a story is another story. When a northern Alaska storyteller completed a story, someone would always say, "You can't leave it standing on one leg." Then he had to tell another tale and sometimes several more. Katherine Scherman was fascinated by the many stories that she heard from Peter Murdoch, the young manager of the Hudson's Bay Company post at Pond Inlet. He had been given the name Aglaktee, "the one who writes," by the local Inuit. When she asked to hear just one more story, he warned her to be careful and told the following tale.

> Once there was a little girl, living with her grandmother. The little girl teased her, "Oh, Grandma, tell me another story." The old woman said, "Once there was a great big lemming, and he was hiding under the tent flap — Ee, there he is now!" The child was so startled that she flew away and became a snow bunting. The old

**118. Josephie Eetook
Kangirsuk c. 1965**
Bear Spirit
**The soul of a hunter could be
lost, possessed by the animal
he was seeking.**

woman cried and her eyes turned red. She flew away to look for the little girl, and became a ptarmigan.

Perhaps we should heed the warning contained in this cautionary fable, but it is difficult to resist the temptation to tell just one more.

Old Satdlage was a Polar Eskimo who always remained silent at the song festivals "in the days when everyone had his own songs which he performed with a chorus of women; when he praised all he found beautiful or condemned what had outraged him." Rasmussen was able to learn his story.

Once when I was a young man, I wanted to compose a song about my village and, for a whole winter evening, I walked up and down in the moonlight, trying to fit words together which would go with a tune I was humming. I did find the words:

excellent words which would convey to my friends the beauty of the mountains and every delightful thing I saw when I went outside and opened my eyes. Pacing up and down on the frozen snow, I became so preoccupied with my thoughts that I quite forgot where I was.

Suddenly, I stop and lift my head. And look! In front of me, the mountain near our village rises higher and steeper than I have ever seen it. It was almost as if it was very slowly growing out of the earth and coming to lean over me, dangerous and threatening. It was then that I heard a voice coming from the air. "Little man!" it cried. "The echo of your words reached me! Do you really think I can be contained in your song?"

I was so frightened that I almost fell over backwards and, in the same moment, all the words I had put together in my song fled from my mind, and I ran home as fast as I could and hid in my hut. Ever since then I have never attempted to put words together. I had become afraid.

We remember the woman who attempted to see the spirit of the singing house and the Cape Dorset artist Niviaksiak who tried to capture the spirit of the bear in his carvings. The Polar Eskimo had carried his search for the perfect words beyond man's depth of understanding. After this experience, Satdlage never again joined the singers. For the rest of his days, he was never able to find the words to celebrate the beauty of his world.

5. Qaudjaqdjuq, Lumak and Kiviung

INUIT STORIES often centre upon individuals who are separated from their communities by choice or by accident and, as a consequence, are not subject to the constraints of rules and normal behaviour. In every area of the arctic, a story is told of a mistreated orphan boy who gains revenge against his tormentors. This legend deals with the universal themes of abandonment and powerlessness, some of the central concerns of Inuit life. Franz Boas recorded the following version of the legend of Qaudjaqdjuq, as told on Baffin Island more than a century ago.

A long time ago there was a poor little orphan boy who had no protector and was maltreated by all the inhabitants of the village. He was not even allowed to sleep in the hut, but lay outside in the cold passage among the dogs, who were his pillows and his quilt. Neither did they give him any meat, but flung old, tough walrus hide at him, which he was compelled to eat without a knife. A young girl was the only one who pitied him. She gave him a very small piece of iron for a knife, but bade him conceal it well or the men would take it from him. Thus he led a miserable life and did not grow at all, but remained poor little Qaudjaqdjuq. He did not even dare to join the plays of the other children, as they also maltreated and abused him on account of his weakness.

When the inhabitants assembled in the singing house Qaudjaqdjuq used to lie in the passage and peep over the threshold. Now and then a man would lift him by the nostrils into the hut and give him the large urine vessel to carry out. It was so large and heavy that he was obliged to take hold of it with both hands and his teeth. As he was frequently lifted by the nostrils they grew to be very large, though he remained small and weak.

At last the man in the moon, who had seen how badly the men behaved towards Qaudjaqdjuq, came down to help him. He harnessed his dog Tirietang to his sledge and drove down. When near the hut he stopped and cried, "Qaudjaqdjuq, come out." Qaudjaqdjuq answered, "I will not come out. Go away!" But when he asked him a second and a third time to come out, he complied, though he was very much frightened. Then the man in the moon went with him to a place where some large boulders were lying about and, having whipped him, asked, "Do you feel stronger now?" Qaudjaqdjuq answered: "Yes, I feel stronger." "Then lift your boulder," said he. As Qaudjaqdjuq was not yet able to lift it, he gave him another whipping, and now all of a sudden he began to grow, the feet first becoming of an extraordinary size. Again the man in the moon asked him: "Do you feel stronger now?" Qaudjaqdjuq answered: "Yes, I feel stronger"; but as he could not yet lift the stone he was whipped once more, after which he had attained a very great strength and lifted the boulder as if it were a small pebble. The man in the moon said: "That will do. Tomorrow morning I shall send three bears; then you may show your strength."

He returned to the moon, but Qaudjaqdjuq, who had now become

Qaudjaqdjuaq (the big Qaudjaqdjuq), returned home tossing the stones with his feet and making them fly to the right and to the left. At night he lay down again among the dogs to sleep. Next morning he awaited the bears and, indeed, three large animals soon made their appearance, frightening all the men, who did not dare to leave the huts.

Then Qaudjaqdjuaq put on his boots and ran down to the ice. The men who looked out of the window hole said, "Look here, is not that Qaudjaqdjuq? The bears will soon make way with him." But he seized the first by its hind legs and smashed its head on an iceberg, near which it happened to stand. The other one fared no better; the third, however, he carried up to the village and slew some of his persecutors with it. Others he pressed to death with his hands or tore off their heads crying: "That is for abusing me; that is for maltreating me." Those whom he did not kill ran away, never to return. Only a few who had been kind to him while he had been poor little Qaudjaqdjuq were spared, among them the girl who had given him the knife. Qaudjaqdjuaq lived to be a great hunter and travelled all over the country, accomplishing many exploits.

Despite the popularity of this legend, the mistreatment of orphans was commented on by many observers of Inuit ways. In 1902, Rasmussen observed the struggle of the Polar Eskimo boy Kajoranguaq to stay alive after his foster mother had died. The story of his proud courage was told admiringly by the outsider. "During some of the snowstorms that raged shortly after he was homeless he had had difficulty in keeping himself alive until he discovered an old ruined building which had been altered into a shelter for a puppy. There, he said, he was very comfortable. . . . He could not have been more than ten years old at the outside, but he manifested already, like a true scion of Eskimos, the passions of his race, loving, beyond all else, the drum songs of his fathers. And he was always singing when he was alone. . . . The day Mikissoq, his foster mother, died I saw him up on the plain behind the tents. He was singing drum songs with a vigour and a delight that surpassed even his wont, and his little face beamed. He beat time to his singing on a little tin box and all his movements were exuberant: his foster mother was dead and it was her illness that had made him homeless."

One decade later, Peter Freuchen objected forcefully to the fate of the Cape York orphan boy Qupagnuk who was always hungry, wore castoff clothing and slept in the entrance tunnels of abandoned snowhouses. Sometimes he was reduced to fighting with the dogs for bits of walrus hide and meat. The boy's real name was Ungaraluk ("the little harpoon") but he was called Qupagnuk ("the snow starling") since "like that little bird he had to pick up a little to eat where it was found." As always, Freuchen was listened to patiently, but he was then told by Qoluqtanguaq in explanation, "Pita, you speak both wisely and at the same time like the newborn child you are in this country! An orphan who has a hard time should never be pitied, for he is merely being hardened to a better life. Look, and you will see that the greatest chief hunters living here have all been orphans." Qoluqtanguaq pointed to Qisunguaq, who as a child was left starving at a time of famine but learned to go hungry longer than people thought was possible and to survive the most cruel cold. Angutidluarssuk spent a miserable childhood but could now do without sleep longer than any other man, and no animal was safe when he was hunting. At eight years of age, Iggianguaq was forced to fend for himself. As a result, he had not grown to normal size but never tired, and he had become the greatest bear hunter and one of the best singers in Greenland. In his turn, Freuchen listened patiently to these stories, yet, true to his own values, he insisted on taking Qupagnuk back with him to Thule.

The struggles of Kajoranguaq, Qupagnuk and the others indicate that Qaudjaqdjuq's trials were not very far removed from ordinary experience. The legend of Qaudjaqdjuq (or Koujeyuk, Kudjuakjuak, Kagssagssuk) is a story about maturing by accepting and enduring hardships. Strength was believed to come from the ability to withstand suffering and deprivation. As recently as the 1950s, the anthropologist Jean Malaurie observed the treatment of an orphan boy among the Caribou Eskimo. "In the central Canadian Arctic, I once stumbled over an orphan. The poor shivering creature was huddled in the *katak* [entrance]; he did not even have the right to share the warmth of family life inside the igloo, only a few feet from his bed. Sitting in the dark passageway, after the others had finished their meal, he ate whatever scraps they chose to leave for him." Malaurie recognized that these hardships were a test, and if an orphan overcame these trials he would be accepted as the best of men.

In the legend of Kagssagssuk as told in Greenland and recorded by Knud Rasmussen, the mistreated orphan boy appeals for help to the Master of

119. Jonasi Naluiyuk   Salluit 1978
Dog with Human Face
The mistreated orphan boy appeals for help to the Master of Strength, who appears in a monstrous form with the face of a human being and a body like an enormous dog.

Strength, who appears in a monstrous form with the face of a human being and a body like an enormous dog. The Master of Strength winds Kagssagssuk up in his tail and hurls him across the ground. Looking back, the boy finds behind him a lot of toys scattered on the ground. The Master of Strength exclaims, "That's why you cannot grow." This is repeated several times until no more toys fall out and the Master of Strength says, "Now no human being can harm you any longer." Unlike Sedna who dreamed of a life without hardships, the orphan boy accepts the difficulties of life. By doing this, he becomes a full member of the human community.

One of the most important legends used to convey Inuit values and beliefs is the timeless story of Lumak, another legend of cruelty, abandonment and vengeance. This is told in many ways—from isolated episodes and fragments to lengthy myths that would take several hours to relate. A very brief version is recorded by James Houston to explain the theme of a 1960 Cape Dorset print.

> The old artist, Kiakshuk, tells the familiar Eskimo legend of the wicked woman who wished to rid herself of her blind husband. She guided him out to the edge of the ice and had him cast his harpoon at a whale which she assured him was only a small seal. As he harpooned it, he heard it blow, and leaped back nimbly, knowing that a whale would be too heavy for him to hold. The wicked woman's legs became entangled in the line and she was dragged into the water. People say that she has been seen recently around Dorset, crying out in anguish as she is pulled forever in the wake of the whale.

As we read a detailed version of the Lumak myth written by Davidialuk, we must imagine a cold igloo in the depths of winter lit by the unsteady flame of a seal oil lamp and the northern lights flickering through the ice window, all occupants held spellbound by the familiar story and the skill of the storyteller.

> A long time ago, many Inuit were living in Arvilik. Since there were so many in that place, some left to look for better hunting grounds. They left only three people in the camp—a mother with her son and daughter. The people intended to return later for these three but the ice melted and they could not get back. In spring, the son developed snowblindness, which was very painful. It was getting hot and the ice window of their igloo melted. Still expecting to be picked up, they lived on in the igloo with no window.
>
> A polar bear came to the place where the igloo had been and the mother prepared the arrow tip for her blind son, helping him to point it towards the window. He shot and killed the bear but his mother told him: "Ukirk is the one who was shot with the arrow." (Ukirk was the name they called their dog.) The blind boy was sure he had heard the roar of a bear and so he said to his mother: "It sounded like a large animal." He did not believe that it was the dog he had shot. His own mother was tricking him. He remembered well the sound of a wounded bear from his old hunting days before he was blind.
>
> The bear had died a distance from the igloo and the mother and daughter went after it, leaving the blind boy alone for a long while. They made a new igloo near the bear. The blind boy thought that they would be cutting up the bear which he'd shot. They had never left him for so long before. The sister would come to see him from time to time, bringing him secret bits of food. She could not stay very

120. Manasie Akpaliapik Arctic Bay 1982 *Three Stories*
When he made this sculpture, Manasie had the loon and the mother from the Lumak
legend in mind. He learned that others saw an angakoq invoking a bird spirit and some
saw Sedna and her bird husband. Manasie said that he preferred the other
interpretations to his own.

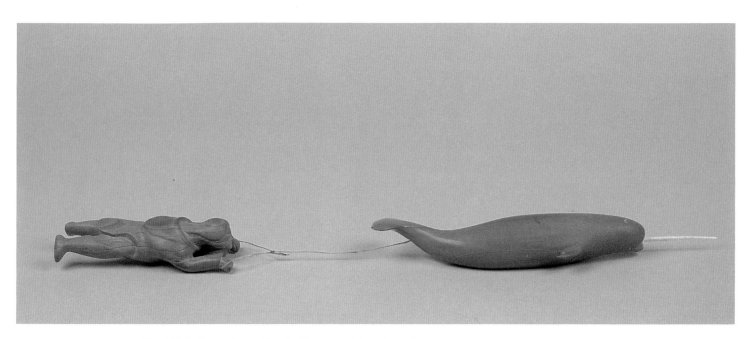

121. Bob Barnabus Arctic Bay c. 1975 *Lumak*
"You can sometimes hear the mother. She says, 'Lumaa, Lumaa, Lumaa. I used to pick
leaves and eat them.' She is sometimes visible for a moment as the whale drags her
about the sea."

long with her brother for fear that the mother would think she was telling about the polar bear. The mother told her to give some meat to her brother but to tell him it was dog meat. The blind boy knew, of course, the taste of bear meat but he did not say anything.

When it became really warm, the igloo caved in with the boy inside alone. The days became longer and every two or three days, his sister would come with food, saying, as she had been instructed, "Here is some dog meat."

The birds came and the blind boy would call out to them, saying: "Make me see again." He was turning to the animals for help. He knew that if it weren't for his sister bringing him food, he would be dead. One day when he was calling out to the birds for help, he heard a loon flying overhead. It sounded then as though someone were trying to get inside the igloo. He could hear singing. Two loons had come in. One asked: "Are you afraid to go under the water?!!"

The boy replied: "I am not afraid if it means I will see again."

The other loon then asked: "Are you afraid to get dressed?"
Again, the boy replied that he was not afraid if it would help him to regain his sight. He got dressed and the two loons walked him to the water. The loons, again enquiring as to whether he was afraid, told him to take his clothes off. When he was naked, they took hold of his legs and dipped him into the water head first. The loons had told him to wiggle his legs when he needed to come up for air. But when he did this, they wouldn't let him up for a long time.

They put him into the water twice and the second time he was in for a long while. They were far from Arvilik when they pulled him up on the land. They put him in the water again and wouldn't let him up for air even when he swallowed water and was breathing bubbles. When they finally let him up, they made him stand and get dressed. In this way he regained his sight. The loons told him to go to his mother as if he were still blind.

He approached his mother, pretending to feel with his hands. With out-stretched arms, he approached her, shouting: "Where do I go?" Even though he was shouting like that, the mother and daughter refused to say anything. He walked towards the bearskin which had been set out to dry. He was thinking of a way to revenge himself with his mother. "Maybe I should make her work very hard?" Seeing the bearskin he felt very angry about the way his mother had treated him. His mother, thinking him still blind, did not offer him anything to eat. Later, when she found out that he could see, she was ashamed and began to treat him very well. She was embarrassed about the bearskin.

He said, "Sister, I wish you would carry me to the seashore! Take me by the hand." The girl took him to the seashore and the boy told her to make an inuk-shuk for him to use as a guide and then to leave him. "I will walk back by myself."

Alone, he started to make a harpoon for he no longer had any of his old hunting equipment. It was summer and one could hunt for harp seals or whales. The boy went to ask his mother to come help him pull in the whale he hoped to harpoon. He waited to hear the breathing of a big whale before shooting his harpoon, but the mother urged him to try for a small whale which would not be difficult for her to pull. She said: "In the stomach! In the stomach! Now! Now! Take that small one! I cannot pull the big one!"

His mother's words made him want to harpoon the largest whale in the sea. He tied the harpoon line around her waist, thinking he would pull with her. Then, although there were small ones, he harpooned the largest whale that came near. He started pulling with his mother and the harpoon line didn't snap. It was firmly imbedded in the whale and so the boy released his mother, to be dragged away by the whale. She was running fast, so fast that her boots resounded on the rocks and her parka tail was flying in the wind behind her. The whale dragged her underwater to the place where whales live.

You can sometimes hear the mother. She says, "Lumaa, Lumaa, Lumaa. I used to pick leaves and eat them." She is sometimes visible for a moment as the whale drags her about the sea.

The brother and sister, left to live alone, had children which populated that place. One of their children, who became a religious fanatic, predicted that they would be eaten by animals. His prediction came true, for they were all eaten by whales. People lived long in those days. The blind boy lived to see his children's children. His descendants wanted to keep this story alive. So finally, here ends the story of that family.

Kiakshuk and Davidialuk tell the legend as an account of real events. The land of Arvilik is not an imaginary location but instead refers to the Ottawa Islands in Hudson Bay. These islands lie about 120 kilometres offshore from Povungnituk and are occasionally visible from the hills along the coastline. The story describes an initiation into manhood and autonomy, symbolized by the killing of the bear and the gaining of vision. More significantly, the legend describes an initiation into the mysteries of life. The blind boy experiences hunger, loneliness and deprivation until his helping spirits appear. The core of the story is the boy's determined cry, "I will see again." He finds the resources within himself to emerge from darkness, to conquer fear and despair. "I am not afraid if it means I will see again." Like the angakoqs in their initiations, he willingly undergoes suffering to the limits of endurance in order to gain the gift of sight.

The legends of Qaudjaqdjuq and Lumak are both stories of vengeance, an accepted custom and even a moral obligation in the Inuit system of justice. Rasmussen recorded some remarkable examples of this practice. He travelled for a time with Inugtuk, a Netsilik hunter who had obtained his wife by murdering her husband Pujataq. At the same time, Inugtuk adopted two sons of the man he had killed. According to Rasmussen, "the whole family now lived together in the greatest harmony, and there seemed to be real affection between them all round—which was the more remarkable as the two lads would, on arriving at man's estate, be expected to take vengeance for the murder of their father." The Caribou Eskimo angakoq Igjugarjuk was more careful to avoid the possibility of vengeance when he acquired his first wife Kivkarjuk from her unwilling family. Igjugarjuk and his brother lay in wait outside her family's igloo and shot her father, mother, brothers and sisters (seven or eight people) until only Kivkarjuk was left alive. In 1910, it was necessary for Rasmussen to use his considerable persuasive powers to convince the brother of Uisaakassak not to fulfil his obligation to seek revenge against the murderers Sigluk and Uutaaq (Odark).

Both legends also focus on another central concern of Inuit life, the rules governing the sharing of food. The people in the stories deny proper food to the helpless orphan and the blind boy even when food was abundant. In doing this, they put themselves outside the protection of the wisdom inherited from the ancestors and encoded in the ancient rules. Before he gained experience in Inuit ways, Peter Freuchen made the mistake of thanking a hunter who gave him a generous gift of several hundred pounds of walrus meat. He was told by old Soqqaq never to thank anyone for meat and was given a very convincing explanation of this custom.

> Up in our country we are human! And since we are human we help each other. We don't like to hear anybody say thanks for that. If I get something today, you may get it tomorrow. Some men never kill anything because they are seldom lucky or they may not be able to run or row as fast as others. Therefore they would feel unhappy to have to be thankful to their fellows all the time. And it would not be fun for the big hunter to feel that other men were constantly humbled by him. Then his pleasure would die. Up here we say that by gifts one makes slaves, and by whips one makes dogs.

"Since we are human we help each other." By not following this most fundamental of all laws, life loses all predictability. Disasters will almost certainly follow, even to the extent of the loss of human identity.

Every mythology can be interpreted as an imaginative history describing the journey of a people through time. Very often, this is represented by an account of an actual journey, a migration or a quest. In western literature, paradigm examples are the Odyssey, Exodus and Don Quixote, among many others. In the Inuit oral tradition, the myth of Kiviung (Kivioq, Kiviuk, Keeveeok, Giviok) tells the story of an epic journey that explores the boundaries of the human world. As in the legends of Qaudjaqdjuq and Lumak, the account recorded by Franz Boas begins with a story of the mistreatment of a child.

> An old woman lived with her grandson in a small hut. As she had no husband and no son to take care of her and the boy, they were very poor, the boy's clothing being made of skins of birds which they caught in snares. When the boy would come out of the hut and join his playfellows, the men would laugh at him and tear his outer garment. Only one man, whose name was Kiviung, was kind to the young boy; but he could not protect him from the others. Often the lad came to his grandmother crying and weeping, and she always consoled him and each time made him a new garment. She entreated the men to stop teasing the boy and tearing his clothing, but they would not listen to her prayer. At last she got angry and swore she would take revenge upon his abusers, and she could easily do so, as she was a great angakoq.
>
> She commanded her grandson to step into a puddle which was on the floor of the hut, telling him what would happen and how he should behave. As soon as he stood in the water the earth opened and he sank out of sight, but the next moment he rose near the beach as a yearling seal with a beautiful skin and swam about lustily.
>
> The men had barely seen the seal when they took to their kayaks, eager to secure the pretty animal. But the transformed boy quickly swam away, as his grandmother had told him, and the men continued in pursuit. Whenever he rose to breathe he took care to come up behind the kayaks, where the men could not get at him with their harpoons; there, however, he splashed and dabbled in order to attract their attention and lure them on. But before any one could turn his

kayak he had dived again and swam away. The men were so interested in the pursuit that they did not observe that they were being led far from the coast and that the land was now altogether invisible.

Suddenly, a gale arose; the sea foamed and roared and the waves destroyed or upset their frail vessels. After all seemed to be drowned the seal was again transformed into the lad, who went home without wetting his feet. There was nobody now to tear his clothing, all his abusers being dead.

Only Kiviung, who was a great angakoq and had never abused the boy, had escaped the wind and waves. Bravely he strove against the wild sea, but the storm did not abate. After he had drifted for many days on the wide sea, a dark mass loomed up through the mist. His hope revived and he worked hard to reach the supposed land. The nearer he came, however, the more agitated did the sea become, and he saw that he had mistaken a wild, black sea, with raging whirlpools, for land. Barely escaping he drifted again for many days, but the storm did not abate and he did not see any land. Again he saw a dark mass looming up through the mist, but he was once more deceived, for it was another whirlpool which made the sea rise in gigantic waves.

At last the storm moderated, the sea subsided, and at a great distance he saw the land. Gradually, he came nearer and following the coast he at length spied a stone house in which a light was burning. He landed and entered the house. Nobody was inside but an old woman whose name was Arnaitiang. She received him kindly and at his request pulled off his boots, slippers, and stockings and dried them on the frame hanging over the lamp. Then she went out to light a fire and cook a good meal.

When the stockings were dry, Kiviung tried to take them from the frame in order to put them on, but as soon as he extended his hand to touch them the frame rose out of his reach. Having tried several times in vain, he called Arnaitiang and asked her to give him back the stockings. She answered: "Take them yourself; there they are; there they are" and went out again. The fact is she was a very bad woman and wanted to eat Kiviung.

Then he tried once more to take hold of his stockings, but with no better result. He called again for Arnaitiang and asked her to give him the boots and stockings, whereupon she said: "Sit down where I sat when you entered my house; then you can get them." After that she left him again. Kiviung tried it once more, but the frame rose as before and he could not reach it.

Now he understood that Arnaitiang meditated mischief; so he summoned his tornaq, a huge white bear, who arose roaring from under the floor of the house. At first Arnaitiang did not hear him, but as Kiviung kept on conjuring the spirit came nearer and nearer to the surface, and when she heard his loud roar she rushed in trembling with fear and gave Kiviung what he had asked for. "Here are your boots," she cried; "here are your slippers; here are your stockings. I'll help you put them on." But Kiviung would not stay any longer with this horrid witch and did not even dare to put on his boots, but took them from Arnaitiang and rushed out of the door. He had barely escaped when it clapped violently together and just caught the tail of his jacket, which was torn off. He hastened to his kayak without once stopping to look behind and paddled away. He had only gone a short distance before Arnaitiang, who had recovered from her fear, came out swinging her glittering woman's knife and threatening to kill him. He was nearly frightened to death and almost upset his kayak. However, he managed to balance it again and cried in answer, lifting up his spear: "I shall kill you with my spear." When

122. Anonymous   Coppermine c. 1975 *Bear Mother*
Animals were believed to have many human attributes. This anthropomorphic bear
nurtures humankind.

Arnaitiang heard these words she fell down terror stricken and broke her knife. Kiviung then observed that it was made of a thin slab of fresh water ice.

He traveled on for many days and nights, following the shore. At last he came to a hut, and again a lamp was burning inside. As his clothing was wet and he was hungry, he landed and entered the house. There he found a woman who lived all alone with her daughter. Her son-in-law was a log of driftwood which had four boughs. Every day about the time of low water they carried it to the beach and when the tide came in it swam away. When night came again it returned with eight large seals, two being fastened to every bough. Thus the timber provided its wife, her mother and Kiviung with an abundance of food. One day, however, after they had launched it as they had always done, it left and never returned.

After a short interval Kiviung married the young widow. Now he went sealing every day himself and was very successful. As he thought of leaving some day, he was anxious to get a good stock of mittens [that his hands might keep dry during the long journey? — Boas]. Every night after returning from hunting he pretended to have lost his mittens. In reality he had concealed them in the hood of his jacket.

After awhile the old woman became jealous of her daughter, for the new husband of the latter was a splendid hunter and she wished to marry him herself. One day when he was away hunting, she murdered her daughter, and in order to deceive him she removed her daughter's skin and crept into it, thus changing her shape into that of the young woman. When Kiviung returned, she went to meet him, as it had been her daughter's custom, and without exciting any suspicion. But when he entered the hut and saw the bones of his wife he at once became aware of the cruel deed and of the deception that had been practiced and fled away.

He traveled on for many days and nights, always following the shore. At last he again came to a hut where a lamp was burning. As his clothing was wet and he was hungry, he landed and went up to the house. Before entering it occurred to him that it would be best to find out first who was inside. He therefore climbed up to the window and looked through the peep hole. On the bed sat an old woman, whose name was Aissivang [spider]. When she saw the dark figure before the window she believed it was a cloud passing the sun, and as the light was insufficient to enable her to go on with her work she got angry. With her knife she cut away her eyebrows, ate them, and did not mind the dripping blood, but sewed on. When Kiviung saw this he thought that she must be a very bad woman and turned away.

Still he traveled on days and nights. At last he came to a land which seemed familiar to him and soon he recognized his own country. He was very glad when he saw some boats coming to meet him. They had been on a whaling excursion and were towing a great carcass to the village. In the bow of one of them stood a stout young man who had killed the whale. He was Kiviung's son, whom he had left as a small boy and who was now grown up and had become a great hunter. His wife had taken a new husband, but now she returned to Kiviung.

"Only Kiviung, who was a great angakoq and had never abused the boy, had escaped the wind and waves." Through his knowledge of himself and the spirit world, Kiviung was able to escape from all dangers.

The myth of Kiviung is an archaic collection of episodes, and it is difficult to reconstruct its meaning after the passage of centuries. The various encounters represent tests of Kiviung's powers as an angakoq in which he is tempted and challenged to give up his human identity. A common magic feat of the angakoqs in their performances was to make the clothes on the drying rack move and

123. Paulassie Kuniliusie   Broughton Island 1982   *Shaman's Hand*
Almost a spirit himself, the shaman's hand declares that he is human in the realm of the spirits.

dance about for no apparent reason. The bad woman Aissivang cutting away her eyebrows is probably a reference to shamanic healing. People suffering from headaches and other illnesses were bled by the angakoqs by cutting the skin above their eyebrows. Aissivang first sees Kiviung as a dark figure before the window and believes that it is a cloud passing the sun. This incident announces Kiviung as an angakoq or, in the secret shamanic language, a *tarijoq*, "one who makes it into a shadow." An apprentice shaman was *tarijunulertoq*, "one who is on the way towards making himself a shadow." The incident also reveals Aissivang as an angakoq since she is able to see Kiviung's shadow. Shamans were believed to have the ability to recognize other angakoqs.

Kiviung's anxiety to get a "good stock of mittens" is motivated more by their use in shamanic rituals than to keep his hands dry as Boas weakly suggests. Mittens were worn as protections against evil spirits. They represented the humanity of the angakoq in his confrontation with the spirit world. An incident recorded by Diamond Jenness indicates this symbolic significance.

> Not many years ago what seems to have been an epidemic of some kind carried off a great many Eskimos in and around Bathurst Inlet. Ilatsiak told me that close to the shore there was a large rock set up by men long ago among a number of small ones. Round this rock he fastened a line, attaching the other end to his belt. Then he spoke to the stone, saying that he did not wish to die, and asking it to preserve his life. When the prayer was ended he gathered six pairs of mittens — two for himself, two for his wife, and two for his adopted son — and with them in his hands he approached the rock and tied them round it as an offering. In consequence he and his family were preserved when others perished.

Among the Igloolik Eskimo, a pregnant woman never went outside without her mittens on. When driving out evil spirits, an angakoq stood with head towards the sky, eyes closed, hands together and always wearing mittens. Metaphorically, mittens protected the prime symbols of human identity. An Igloolik version of the myth of Kivioq has an ending that emphasizes the significance of the hands of the angakoq. They have been almost worn away from the fatigue of his journey.

> When he recognized his village, he paddled inwards and his hands were nearly gone and when he became visible, his wife exclaimed: "It is my husband alone whose hands are going away!" People said to her: "Your husband has long been dead!" But she replied: "It is my husband, since his hands are tired." Thus her husband at last came home to her again, and he distributed beads to his fellow villagers.

After his long absence, Kivioq's wife was just able to recognize him by seeing his hands. It was by losing her hands that Sedna broke her connection with the human world.

One key to interpreting the myth of Kiviung may be the repeated phrase "He travelled on for many days and nights, following the shore." The large rock described by Ilatsiak was set up as a landmark "close to the shore" by men long ago. In the version of the legend recorded by Lucien Turner, the orphan boy Koujeyuk revealed his new powers by "picking up rocks and tossing them along the shore until the character of the water's edge was entirely changed." In the legend of Lumak, the blind boy asks his sister to take him to the seashore and to make an inukshuk for him to use as a guide. His cruel mother meets her retribution on the shore. In all three legends, the shore represents the boundary between the human and spirit worlds. This powerful image is made explicit in a ritual recorded by Franz Boas. "Storm and bad weather, when lasting a long time

124. Nelson Takkiruq   Gjoa Haven 1990   *Kiviuq's Journey*
The greatest angakoq Kiviuq experienced many adventures in his journey of discovery.
He proved himself the master of land, sea and air.

and causing want of food, are conjured by making a large whip of seaweed, step-
ping to the beach, and striking out in the direction whence the wind blows, at
the same time crying *taba* (it is enough)." In the great creation myth, Sedna and
her father meet their fates as they attempt to return to the shore.

By following the shore in his journey, Kiviung always keeps the human
world in sight. Gontran de Poncins described one arduous journey by dogteam
in words that echo this image from the story of Kiviung: "To reach Pelly Bay we
had to cross an arm of the sea. The distance straight across was a mere fifty miles,
but the Eskimos never go straight across: they follow the coast, their object being
always to keep certain landmarks in sight." In the myth of Kiviung, the men of
the village are lost when they pursue the yearling seal so far from the coast that
the land becomes invisible. Soqqaq's accusation against the Big Liar Uisaakassak
when he returned from New York was that he had been far away and no longer
knew the truth. He had forgotten the familiar landmarks of the human world.

There are many episodes omitted in the Boas account that occur in other
versions. In the Bathurst Inlet region, the storyteller Karonak told Raymond de
Coccola that nobody knew where Kiviuk came from, although he had been seen

125. Seetee Natsiapik   Broughton Island c. 1970   *Hand and Spirit*
A sculpture that expresses the separation of body and spirit. The angakoq has left his
body to travel to the spirit world, but he retains the hand as a sign of his humanity. The
sculpture may also represent Sedna's terror at her fate, the loss of her human identity.

126. Luke Nuliayok   Gjoa Haven c. 1978   *Kiviuq's Journey*
Kiviuq showed his mastery of nature by riding the whale to the spirit world without
becoming a spirit himself.

in Taheriuk. "Some claimed he came from the Bottom of the Sea; others from
the Land of the Day." In his recounting of the legend, Karonak focussed on
Kiviuk's encounter with a sorceress in her igloo.

> Once they were both inside, she asked Kiviuk to undress and place his clothing on
> the drying rack above the blubber lamp. Then she took her *ulon* [woman's knife]
> and told him she was going out to fetch more blubber for the stone lamp.
> Unbeknown to Kiviuk, the woman was a sorceress who intended to make a big
> fire in which to cook Kiviuk and eat him.
>   Looking around the igloo, Kiviuk saw many human skulls, all clean-picked
> without a trace of flesh on them. To his added amazement, one of the skulls
> opened its mouth and said: "Run away, run away! Or the sorceress will eat you
> when she returns. Look at us! She devoured our bodies. Nothing is left of us, but
> our bones. Run, run for your life!"

When Kiviuk tried to grab his clothing off the rack, he could not do so because they were jumping up and down and sideways. Fortunately Kiviuk had a helpful spirit — Orkpik, the Big Owl — whom he invoked at once: "Orkpik, Orkpik, fly over here and help me!" The Bird Spirit flew in through the opening in the roof and with wings pushed Kiviuk's clothing into his arms. Dressing as speedily as he could, Kiviuk darted through the door and sprinted down the sloping seashore to his kayak.

"Nothing is left of us, but our bones." If an angakoq failed to return from his dangerous journey to the spirit world, nothing would be left behind except his skeleton. The sorceress chased after Kiviuk but, failing to catch him, she threw her *ulon* after him. As it skidded over the water, it created all the ice on the seas, the lakes and the rivers. "Before Kiviuk met the sorceress, there had never been ice on our waters."

In Karonak's telling of the myth, the helping spirit descending from the spirit world recalls similar images that occur in the stories of the orphan boy and the blind boy. It also recalls images from Christianity and even the *deus ex machina* of Greek drama. An almost universal symbol of wisdom, the owl sees

127. Harold Qarliksaq
Baker Lake c. 1975 *Bird Spirit*
At the moment the angakoq's spirit was released from his body, a bird could be seen flying away from the igloo carrying his soul to the spirit world.

128. Louie Qingnaqtuq   Gjoa Haven 1991   *Skeletal Drummer*
Leaving his bones behind, the angakoq has departed on the spirit journey, not knowing if
he will be able to find his body again.

ahead and behind and can find its way in darkness. The three legends reminded the listeners that everything in life was observed by the unseen forces and they reminded them that their own experiences were a spiritual journey, a struggle to transcend material concerns. One nameless Inuit song recorded by Rasmussen describes in the simplest terms what is important in life.

And I think over again
My small adventures
When with a shore wind I drifted out
In my kayak
And thought I was in danger.
My fears,
Those small ones
That I thought so big,
For all the vital things
I had to get and to reach.

And yet, there is only
One great thing,
The only thing:
To live to see in huts and on journeys
The great day that dawns,
And the light that fills the world.

129. Paulassie Karpik   Pangnirtung
Visionary Journey
"He traveled on for many days and nights, always following the shore." Kiviung spends a lifetime confronting the spirits, other angakoqs and the mysterious forces of nature. Unmoved by all dangers and temptations, he struggles to retain his human identity.

130. Jacoposie Tiglik   Pangnirtung c. 1975   *Soul Flight*
In a dream or an ecstatic trance, the inua of the angakoq is released to take flight to the
spirit world.

131. Isaac Panigayak   Gjoa Haven 1990   *Two Worlds*
Like the Roman god Janus, the angakoq looks into the past and the future and into the
worlds of the real and the imagined. His magic words and bird helping spirits travel to the
ends of the earth.

Every hunter must accept the dangers of drifting out from the shore, away from the human world. But he must always keep in mind the "one great thing, the only thing." The mysterious contests with natural and supernatural forces can be interpreted as nothing less than Kiviung's struggle to be human. His reward for prevailing in this struggle was to complete the cycle of life by returning to his home. Like the orphan Qaudjaqdjuq who survives to become a great hunter and the blind boy who lives to see his children's children, Kiviung rediscovers himself in the son who has become a great hunter. After their trials, all three find the meaning of life in ordinary human values.

Every teller of the myth of Kiviung insists on the humanity of the central figure. In a 1979 drawing *Kiviuk and the Grizzly*, the Baker Lake artist Oonark wrote an accompanying text on the border. Her story begins, "There were some birds playing in the water. Kiviuk watched. As he could be anything, he decided to be a person. . . ." The great angakoq explores the domains of earth, sea and air like the birds playing in the water, but he chooses to retain his human identity. He escapes from the wind and the waves to return to the human world. Another Baker Lake artist, Victoria Mamnguqsualuk (Oonark's daughter), is well known for her drawings inspired by the legend of Keeveeok, although she has admitted, "I heard this story as a child but I don't know the ending because I always fell asleep." For Inuit children, the stories of Qaudjaqdjuq, Lumak and Kiviung very often ended in dreams.

When he visited the Netsilik Eskimo, Rasmussen learned that Kiviung's story does not have an ending. There he was asked if he had seen Kivioq in his travels. When he pretended not to know the story, he was told, "Kivioq is an inuk, a man like ourselves, but a man with many lives. He is from times when the ice never laid itself on the sea up here by our coasts." They had heard that Kivioq had gone to live in the land of the white men where he is living his last life. In former times, when he came to the end of one life, he fell into a deathlike sleep. When he awoke, he began a new life. The Netsilik storyteller ended by saying, "Since Kivioq settled among the white men, we know no more to tell about him. All we know is that he is still alive and that before he ends his last life he will once more see the Inuit, his countrymen, and his native land."

6. My Sleep Is Dreamless

SINCE THE BEGINNING of the modern period of Inuit art, there has been a continuing debate concerning its meaningfulness. Some critics have maintained that the art phenomenon has been primarily a calculated commercial activity inspired by outside influences with little connection to a vanished way of life. These observers have an appealing romantic image of a lost culture that was totally self-reliant and free from external pressures. In this imagined culture, every activity and object was believed to be infused with a genuine spiritual significance. Every legend and myth was accepted as true. Every shamanic performance was sincerely motivated. Judged against this standard, the products of contemporary artists will inevitably be found wanting. Clearly, these artists do not live in an autonomous, coherent culture dealing on equal terms with external influences. In the debate, epithets such as "illustrations," "souvenir carvings," "exploitative charlatans" and worse have been used to dismiss the artistic significance of almost all of the modern production.

It must be admitted that there have been some false starts in the development of modern Inuit art. One example is the first production of graphic art at Holman Island in the early 1960s. Under the supervision of the local Catholic missionary, sealskin tapestries were produced depicting human figures wearing Roman togas in intricate biblical scenes with border designs of grapes and tropical leaves. Armand Tagoona, a Baker Lake artist and religious leader, has questioned the inspiration of some Inuit art. "I have seen some drawings in the Craft Shop that have no real source, no history at all, created by the artist from nothing, because there is a rumour that's the kind of thing *qablunaat*, or white people, like. Every time a white person saw a horror figure drawn by an Eskimo, he was fascinated by it, because maybe he believed that Eskimos think that way. I know that in the case of some horror drawings, the artist got the idea first from comic books." Tagoona may not have been aware of similar trends at the same time in the New York art world. More seriously, it could be mentioned that there are many parallels between the conventions of comic books and those of traditional Inuit narratives.

The other side of the argument maintains that Inuit art represents a revival of culturally significant values expressed in a new form. This viewpoint sees a continuity of creative expression by artists very aware of their heritage even while they are experiencing many outside influences. In this view, art activities have helped to reestablish links to the past, connections that had been broken by the intervention of whalers, traders and missionaries and by the secularization of hunting. Despite some of the extreme positions taken in interpreting the recent art production, the argument should focus on the cultural meaning of the new forms in contemporary Inuit society. It cannot be settled without examining that rapidly evolving society in all its complexity and contradictions. Until this is

132. Aisa Amittu   Akulivik 1987   *Old Man's Dream*
It is dangerous to wake a sleeping man since his soul may be on a distant journey. If
woken before his soul returns of its own accord, the man may become sick and die. Aisa
Amittu has borrowed an image from his father Davidialuk; the sinuous forms indicate the
presence of the spirits represented as the northern lights.

done, the evident cultural significance and aesthetic power of much of this art
will continue to present unresolved challenges to all who encounter it. In
Sculpture of the Eskimo, George Swinton points out that this dilemma presents
some advantages; "The absence of limiting art criteria has been a real blessing to
the contemporary Inuit artists, a nightmare to art-studying anthropologists and
an odious bone of contention to traditionalists."

During the Fifth Thule Expedition from 1921-24, Rasmussen made every
attempt to find Inuit groups that had not been significantly influenced by commercial whaling, by fur trading or by missionary activities. He was tirelessly
searching for the people he called our contemporary ancestors. In this effort, he
was never completely successful. With great determination he travelled to one
remote inland community where he expected to find people living in a quite
primitive state. His reaction was surprise and disappointment when he heard

coming from one of their summer tents the unmistakable sounds of a Caruso recording being played on a powerful gramophone. At that point, he expressed the understandable feeling that he was about a hundred years too late. When he reached the Mackenzie Inuit in the western Canadian Arctic, he found prosperous hunters, some of whom were wealthy enough to own motorized schooners. They were temporarily benefitting from recent high prices for the furs they trapped, especially the white arctic fox, which was then in great demand. One opportunist generously offered to describe the local folklore and mythology for a consideration of twenty-five dollars a day. Among all these smart business folk, as Rasmussen described them, he felt that he was an old fossil to be interested in the ancient ways of life.

The old hunter Ikinilik of the Caribou Eskimo explained to Rasmussen the changes that he had seen take place in his lifetime.

> Now that we have firearms it is almost as if we no longer need shamans or taboos, for now it is not so difficult to procure food as in the old days. Then we had to laboriously hunt the caribou at the sacred crossing places, and there the only thing that helped us was the strictly observed taboo in combination with magic words and amulets. Now we can shoot caribou everywhere with our guns, and the result is that we have lived ourselves out of the old customs. We forget our magic words and we scarcely use any amulets now. The young people don't. See, my chest is bare; I haven't got all the bones and grave-goods that the Netsilingmiut hang about them. We forget what we no longer have use for. Even the ancient spirit songs that the great shamans sing together with all the men and women of the village we forget, all the old invocations for bringing Nuliajuk up to earth so that the beasts can be wrested from her — we remember them no more.

Rasmussen describes the many problems he encountered in attempting to learn the secret knowledge of the shamans that Ikinilik claimed had been forgotten. The first reaction was usually denial. "In the evening I ventured to touch on my special subject, and explained to Igjugarjuk, who was famous as an angakoq through the whole of the Barren Grounds, that I was most anxious to learn something of their ideas about life, their religion and folklore. But here I was brought up short. He answered abruptly that he was an ignorant man, knowing nothing of his people and its past; if any had said he was an angakoq, they lied." Another time, Ikinilik told Rasmussen, "Our angakoqs nowadays do not know very much, they only talk a lot, and that is all they can do; they have no special time of study and initiation, and all their power is obtained from dreams, visions or sickness. I once asked a man if he was an angakoq and he answered: 'My sleep is dreamless, and I have never been ill in my life!'"

This denial of knowledge of traditional ways is a culture trait that continues to the present time. In initial contacts, this reaction occurs so frequently that it has been called the *amai* (I don't know) response by Robert Williamson in his studies of the Keewatin Inuit. Other observers of this phenomenon were K. J. Butler and Sheila Butler, who played major roles in the development of the art program in Baker Lake in the late 1960s and the early 1970s. They were intrigued by the depiction of themes taken from shamanism, but K. J. Butler met with some resistance when he attempted to learn more about these sources.

> When I first raised the subject of shamanism in Baker, people would absolutely refuse to discuss it. If you were in a crowd, you would see people leaving the crowd all around; they would translate faultily and the conversation would break down. For the most part, people were not willing to discuss the traditional tales or legends or certainly anything about shamanism if confronted on the subject, but they will put the same material into drawings because there's no Church taboo regarding drawings — and drawings can be incredibly candid.

Dorothy Eber encountered this familiar response when she interviewed old people who had memories of the whalers and whaling stations; "When I first met Anirnik, she frequently drew dramatic mask designs for Cape Dorset's print-making program. There were shamans aboard the *Active* [a Scottish whaling ship], and one day I asked, 'Are those shaman's masks?' Anirnik, a good Anglican, replied, 'Maybe they are . . .' and then changed her mind: 'But I don't think of shamans when I do them.'"

When interviewed by Eber, the Cape Dorset artist Pitseolak Ashoona was also reluctant or unable to explain the sources for her many drawings. She admitted that she became an artist to make money, but she said that she considered herself a real artist.

> Jim Houston told me to draw the old ways, and I've been drawing the old ways and the monsters ever since. We heard that Sowmik ["left-handed," Houston] told the people to draw anything, in any shape and to put a head and face on it. He told the people that this drawing was very good. Some people saw the monsters, somewhere, some place, but I have never seen the monsters I draw. But I keep on drawing these things and, sometimes, when I take Terry [Ryan] a monster drawing, I say, "Perhaps when I die, I'll see these monsters."

Pitseolak claimed that she had forgotten most of the Eskimo legends she had learned as a child. She did remember the one about the blind boy who got back his eyesight when a bird took him on his back and dived with him under the sea three times. "The blind young man lived with his mother who was cruel to him and, when he returned home and she saw he could see, this wicked mother was so frightened she jumped into the sea. Eskimos believe she became a white whale and is there still — they really believe it." Pitseolak also remembered the spirit who lived in the moon. "When I heard that the two men had landed on the moon I wondered what the spirit thought of these two men landing on his land." At the beginning of the interviews, Pitseolak introduced herself by going back to an older way of description. "My name is Pitseolak, the Eskimo word for sea pigeon. When I see pitseolaks over the sea, I say, 'There go those lovely birds — that's me flying.'"

After his initial disappointments, Rasmussen quickly realized that the old beliefs were still powerful despite the newly acquired trappings of civilization. In the inland community where he encountered the Caruso recording, he forgot his disappointment altogether when one of the young men asked him whether seals had horns like the caribou. It was due in large part to the changes that had already occurred that he was able to record the timeless legends and myths, to collect amulets and to ask the angakoqs about their secrets. The traditional cul-

133. Simon Qamanirq   Arctic Bay c. 1965   *Inner Vision*
A small carved head shows the intense concentration of the angakoq as the soul is released from the body.

134. Manasie Akpaliapik   Arctic Bay 1988   *Caribou Shaman*
The angakoq summons his caribou helping spirit before leaving on the soul journey.

135. James Ungalaq   Igloolik 1990   *Mask*
A mask with bear teeth conceals the identity of the angakoq. It shows the pain and fear of the shamanic transformation and the power of the bear.

ture had been altered sufficiently under the pressure of outside influences that, with persistence and sensitive encouragement, many Inuit were able to speak about their beliefs with some degree of freedom and objectivity. However, even with this increased freedom, it can still be a challenge to interpret the work of contemporary artists. K. J. Butler describes very well the problem of attempting to understand one Baker Lake artist renowned for her drawings, prints and tapestries.

> Oonark is hard to translate, they say, "because she talks in circles" — it keeps being the same subject over and over with slightly different modifiers or suffixes or affixes so that she is turning the same subject to many sides and lining them all up in front of you. To the young, it is repetitious; to the old people, it is providing all the necessary information surrounding the subject.

In a world view that does not accept a simple causality but instead sees everything as connected to everything else, talking in circles may be the appropriate way to describe events and explain behaviour. When she was asked one time where the ideas for her drawings came from, Oonark responded, "Don't let them worry you, they are only my dreams."

Forty years before the Fifth Thule Expedition, Franz Boas found that many traditions among the Inuit of Baffin Island had been modified as a result of European influence, but these customs had not yet broken down. There was a continuing strong belief in the many taboos and in the healing powers of the angakoqs. Because of their beliefs, Boas writes that "the Eskimos do not make images of the tornait (spirits) or other supernatural beings in whom they believe." Rasmussen encountered similar views of life. "The earth and everything belonging to it — stones, grass, turf, etc. — are sacred throughout the whole of summer, both at the salmon places and at *nablut* [caribou crossing places]; for this reason alone stone huts must never be built, nor must one ever break stones, pluck grass, or wipe the hands on grass." Until the hold of these beliefs had been weakened, it is evident that the contemporary expression of spirit images in graphic art and sculptures was not possible. It should be noted that these prohibitions were not followed universally. Boas was able to obtain some illustrations of the legend of Qaudjaqdjuq. The Inuit encountered by Rasmussen in Alaska followed very different traditions; "The angakoq, after a visit to the spirit world, endeavours to give a record of what he has seen by carving masks to represent the different faces he has seen, the spirits also being present. He further calls in the aid of others, who carve according to his instructions, producing a great number of remarkable fantastic masks."

At the time that Boas lived in the arctic, there had already been several decades of extensive contact in some regions with the Scottish and American whaling stations. It was common for the whalers in the last century to hire local Inuit to serve as hunters and navigators. It is notable that the Inuit accepted employment in tasks that were closely related to their traditional skills. They were much less successful at repetitive tasks requiring regular hours and punctuality. For a winter's work, the total payment might be a rifle, a small accordion and a provision of food for the hunter's family. One influence of this payment on Inuit traditions is somewhat surprising. In several areas of the Arctic, accordions

136. Omalluq Oshutsiaq   Cape Dorset 1989   *Accordion Player*
"Danasee! Danasee! We love the word that we learned from the whalers a century ago.
The people have always found joy by singing and dancing in the festival house. When we
begin to dance, we never want to stop."

and fiddles obtained from the whaling stations began to replace the caribou skin
drums in their healing rituals and festivals. Some Inuit dances began to resemble
American square dances and Scottish reels. A few decades later, gramophones
and cylinder records were traded for eagerly and used for the old purposes. Are
these examples of cultural breakdown or of cultural adaptability?

Only with the appearance of Christianity were the old beliefs finally abandoned. This was a lengthy process, which in some ways has not been completed

even at the present time. The early missionaries very often found themselves in a contest for influence with the angakoqs. E. W. Hawkes reported that the Labrador Eskimo told the early missionaries that they would listen to them if they knew more about the spirit world than their angakoqs. In 1910 at the beginning of his long career as an Anglican missionary, Archibald Fleming gained an immediate advantage over the local shamans by predicting the arrival of Halley's comet a few days before it became visible. His prediction was received very skeptically. He was asked, "How can the teacher know this? He is very young and not like our angakoqs who have unnatural powers." When the spectacular phenomenon was seen a few nights later, the Inuit were deeply affected by it and clamoured to know how Fleming could have foretold its coming. For years after, the reputation of his great powers preceded him in his extensive arctic travels and contributed greatly to his ability to win converts.

Fleming was once invited to attend a Sedna festival near Lake Harbour on Baffin Island. Only after "prayerful consideration" did he agree to come to "this exhibition of pagan magic and dancing." He wrote that he eventually decided to attend since if he did not "Pitsoolak (the angakoq) might well claim that we were afraid of his powers since he attended our services." Fleming was not the only missionary to be troubled by an uncomfortable parallelism between his activities and those of the angakoqs. The seeming death and rebirth of the angakoq in the Sedna ritual is very reminiscent of the central mystery of the Christian religion. There were many reports of angakoqs returning to life after three or four days in

137. Stephen Alookee   Spence Bay 1976
Wounded Shaman
Angakoqs entered the world of darkness, the realm of death, to find the causes of illness, famine and misfortune. In shamanism, the knife is a reminder of the shaman's initiation when his body was dismembered and reassembled. The angakoq's body is half-human, half-skeleton, showing the duality of the shamanic state.

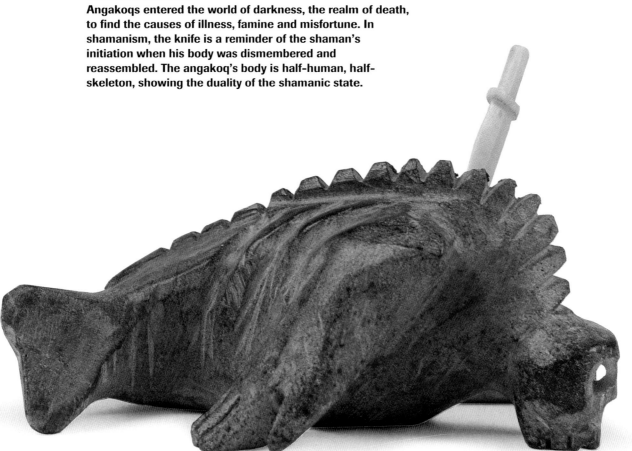

138. Charlie Ugyuk   Spence Bay 1988
Harpooned Shaman
The call to become a shaman was received with fear since the angakoq's life was full of dangers. The common image of an angakoq harpooning himself shows the power over death that he acquires after experiencing great hardships. It also expresses his submission to his fate.

139. Inuksak   Repulse Bay c. 1975
Powerful Shaman
An angakoq enters the spirit of a walrus to visit the mother of the sea animals. Armed with staff and knife as symbols of his shamanic powers, he confronts the most dangerous spirit.

a death-like state. Fleming was also aware that the old beliefs had not been forgotten with the arrival of a new religion. They continued to have a deep influence on behaviour. He recounted a less dramatic incident that echoes Rasmussen's experiences and illustrates the changes that were occurring.

> When I first asked Mary to tell me the meaning of the tattooing on her face and wrists, she said, "I am as one who has forgotten." At first, I thought she had said, "I have forgotten," and knowing that this could not be true I repeated my question. When she said again, "I am as one who has forgotten," I felt rebuked as I realized that with the acceptance of the Christian faith Mary had put away the old beliefs and practices.

Mary and the others were attempting to live in a new way following the example of the missionary they called Inuktakaub, "the new person."

The conversion to Christianity was often very tentative and partial. When he became a Christian, the angakoq Aua realized that he would no longer need his helping spirits. Knowing their value, however, he sent them to his sister who lived on Baffin Island. Raymond de Coccola found that his hard-won influence

140. Isah Sheeg   Povungnituk 1979
Prayer
The humble posture, the emphasis on hands, the bird imagery and the search for an inner vision are elements of Christian iconography that are common to visualizations of spiritual experiences in the traditional beliefs.

141. Anonymous   Iqaluit c. 1960
Bishop
A portrait of an Anglican bishop seeking inspiration, a word that means breath. The reverse of the sculpture presents a deeply felt imaginative vision of the helping spirits of the Christian religion.

could disappear at times of crisis. Once he was accused of causing a virulent epidemic. "Kirluayok (the angakoq) warned us that your medicine could kill us. He said the Spirits of the Sea and Land told him in his dreams that we must avoid touching or receiving anything from you, or we shall die." At another time, Kirluayok told him directly that there was no room in the community for the two of them. As recently as the 1960s, Duncan Pryde believed from his observations that the old ways had a deeper hold than Christian beliefs. "Most Eskimos at Perry River were nominally Anglicans. When the Anglican missionary arrived at the settlement, they would all attend the services but my observation was that they were all pagans. Belief in shamanism and spirits was strong and generations old. Christianity was popular when the missionary was there; the next day he would be gone and his religion with him."

The Catholic missionary Roger Buliard, a contemporary of de Coccola, described a shaman, Kinakia, who made amulets even while fingering a prayer book. He was at a loss to explain the powers that others ascribed to her since to him her amulets looked more like rag dolls than powerful idols. The Inuit were more tolerant or more fearful in accepting both religions. Buliard noted their "natural tendency to regard Christianity as just another, perhaps more powerful, medicine, a better magic than the shaman offers." The missionary failed to realize that Kinakia valued the prayer book that he had given her as a new amulet. One time, Buliard decided to experiment with the Inuit belief system. He threw some large boulders down a cliff after he had been told that this would offend Sila and might cause a storm. When nothing happened, he was told to never kill a raven since that would be certain to bring bad weather. Taking this warning as a challenge, he killed the first raven that he saw. The inevitable result followed. "A few hours later an arctic tornado mowed down every tent in the settlement. The Eskimos smiled knowingly at me, saying nothing, but very much amused and quite superior."

Peter Freuchen observed a revealing incident that illustrates again the conflict between new and old ways. When the sun reappeared for the first time after the winter darkness, it was the custom among the Polar Eskimos to greet its return with bare head and hands. They believed that those who did this would live another year. On one occasion, Freuchen was pleased to participate in this ritual, but a visiting scientist in their group mocked this superstition and refused to "humour the natives in such a stupid fashion." Old Ulugatok from Cape York stopped the visitor and reprimanded him.

> We are only poor, silly people. We have few ways of protecting ourselves for the sake of our children, so we only do as our forefathers have taught us to do. If you need not do the same thing, it is convenient for you, but you should not laugh at us merely because you are stronger. We think that if we do this we shall not die at least until the sun returns next year. Even if this does no good, we enjoy life so much that we do anything to keep it.

It would be difficult to improve on Ulugatok's explanation of the rationality of following the ancient rules and rituals. In Freuchen's experience, it was very unusual for Inuit to contradict or criticize outsiders. He was often told, "They are like newborn children in our country, and it would be below one's dignity to contradict a senseless child." Freuchen also recorded that only the visitor in this small group of travellers did not live to celebrate the sun's return one year later.

During the Fifth Thule Expedition, Therkel Mathiassen stayed in the area of northwest Hudson Bay and northern Baffin Island to study the archaeology of the Tunit people. His research on Southampton Island took a dangerous turn when an angakoq blamed him for the poor hunting and an outbreak of illness, saying that Mathiassen had robbed the graves of the ancestors. After he returned to safety on the mainland, he was present to witness the first arrival of Christianity in the region near Igloolik. In this unusual case, the Inuit acted as their own missionaries. Two recent arrivals, Uming and his son Noqatdlaq, had introduced a primitive form of Christianity. They were fugitives from Pond Inlet on northern Baffin Island where Noqatdlaq had shot a white man, an independent trader who had begun to steal furs at gunpoint. Mathiassen gives the following description of the new religion.

> When we came to Ingnertoq, we saw a white rag on a pole outside the snowhouse and, when we arrived at the place, we were surprised by the inhabitants shaking hands with us; even the tiniest child had to do it. . . . Besides the handshake and the white flag, Uming's religion included abstention from work on Sundays, gathering now and then in his snowhouse and singing hymns which he taught them, and, what is more, the hunters were to bring their booty to him and he would distribute it. His son, the murderer, Noqatdlaq, acted as a sort of assistant priest and did not lift a finger in hunting either. When people arrived at the settlement or departed from it, all the inhabitants gathered and sang a hymn, after which the handshaking commenced; even the dog's paws were taken.

The great attraction of this new religion came from the freedom it offered from the many rules, taboos and fears that governed traditional life. The observance of the ancient rules had been comparatively strict in the Igloolik area since, according to a local tradition, Sedna had met her fate there. As we can see, some new taboos were introduced such as the prohibition of work on Sundays, but these were much less onerous than the previous restrictions. Even the all-important rules for dividing food were abandoned. The two missionaries also decreed that the trading of wives was henceforth forbidden except, of course, for themselves since they were superior beings. The strength of the new beliefs was indicated by Mathiassen's failure when he attempted to trade for an ivory and wood crucifix that one of the recent converts had made. He was told that it was a very powerful amulet and could not be sold. The new faith spread rapidly although it was not accepted universally. Some of the older people were less willing to be convinced.

> In the spring of 1922, when the Igluliks were on a trading journey to Repulse Bay, the handshake, the white flag and the hymns spread to the Aiviliks, many of whom at once went over to the new faith; Aua was converted after his eldest son had dreamt that it was the true faith. Many old people, however, regarded it with skepticism. "Apaq has become a Christian for her food" said old Takornaq of a young woman who, on account of a birth, was under restraint by the many food prohibi-

tions but now enthusiastically took to the new religion and discarded the old taboos.

It was not very long before there was some backsliding from the new beliefs. Peter Freuchen gave an account of some interesting events that occurred one year later. He lived for a time with Uming who conceived the idea that his guest was a model of kindness and wisdom who had come on a divine mission. To all Freuchen's protests and denials, Uming answered, "Great men are always modest."

> During the fall the natives [near Repulse Bay] turned pagan again. They had been Christian for more than a year and it had done them no good — the dogs had come down with distemper just the same. The Eskimos had even gone so far as to hang tiny crosses about the dogs' necks, but it had not helped. Then a young woman remembered that once as a child she had cured a dog by binding pagan amulets around its neck. She was a cautious, clever girl, so now she fastened both a cross and a round piece of wood to several dogs' necks, and the animals recovered. Then, by a scientific system of trial and elimination, they set about to determine which had been responsible for the cure. Half the remaining sick animals were treated with crosses, the rest with the wooden amulets. The dogs wearing the pagan wood recovered. Whereupon the natives returned to the ways of their forefathers, and doubtless remained satisfied until another problem arose.

The Igloolik converts were also becoming more skeptical about the new religion since the weather had been bad all summer. However, Noqatdlaq had recently been sentenced to ten years imprisonment at Stony Mountain Penitentiary in Manitoba for the murder of the white trader. The fact that the government was rewarding him with shelter, food and clothing without any effort on his part was accepted as convincing proof of the benefits to be obtained from the Christian faith.

At about the same time that this unorthodox missionary activity was taking place, another reflection of cultural adaptation was occurring on the opposite coast of Hudson Bay. Robert Flaherty completed his film *Nanook of the North*, now recognized as a landmark documentary of the Inuit way of life. Filmed near present day Inukjuak (then called Port Harrison), it presents a simple narrative of events in the life of the hunter Nanook. The action centres on a journey to a trading post and a dramatic walrus hunt. In one memorable scene, the trader plays a gramophone for Nanook, who is so puzzled and curious about the source of the music that he bites the record. The film was first shown to southern audiences in 1922 in New York where it met an enthusiastic reception.

There has been some criticism of Flaherty's film, claiming that it is not a valid documentary of the Inuit hunting culture but instead an imaginative reconstruction. Among many details that could be mentioned, even the clothing of the actors had to be made from memory since they did not reflect the current trading post clothes. These criticisms are similar to those made of contemporary Inuit art. This art is seen by some as an attempt to recreate ways of life and values that have no current relevance. The making of *Nanook* was a complex and lengthy project, which did have substantial input from the participants. Flaherty recalled a conversation with Nanook that illustrates the difficulties in making the film and in communicating across a cultural divide.

> "Suppose we go," said I, "do you know that you and your men may have to give up making a kill, if it interferes with my film? Will you remember that it is the picture of you hunting the *iviuk* (walrus) that I want and not their meat?"
>
> "Yes, yes, the *aggie* (movie) will come first," earnestly he assured me. "Not a man will stir, not a harpoon will be thrown until you give the sign. It is my word." We shook hands and agreed to start the next day.

The hunter who played the title role in the film was not able to grasp the significance of the project. "He never quite understood why I should have gone to all the fuss and bother of making the 'big aggie' of him—the hunting, yes—but surely everyone knew the Eskimo, and could anything possibly be more common than dogs and sledges and snow houses."

Flaherty's own words describe his ambitious motivations in creating *Nanook of the North* and his other documentary films.

> I am not going to make films about what the white man has made of primitive peoples. . . . what I want to show is the former majesty and character of these people, while it is still possible—before the white man has destroyed not only their character, but the people as well. The urge that I had to make *Nanook* came from the way I felt about these people, my admiration for them; I wanted to tell others about them.

142. **Anonymous   Repulse Bay 1968**
Drum Dance

143. **Regilee Piungituq   Clyde River 1988**

144. **Susan Niurtuq   Baker Lake 1965**

As the caribou skin drum exerts its hypnotic power, the angakoq prepares for the visionary journey. The turned head shows that the shaman is turning away from the human world.

To do this, Flaherty realized that he had to work in an entirely different way. His aim was to show the Inuit "not from the civilized point of view, but as they saw themselves, as 'we, the people'." There is no doubt about the attitudes of present day Inuit to *Nanook*. At the request of the Inuit Tapirisat (Brotherhood) of Canada, the film was shown throughout northern Canada in June 1979 using the Anik B satellite. The common reaction was great pride in the dignity and fortitude of their ancestors. This incident illustrates again that contemporary Inuit have the ability to adapt new ways and modern technology to their current needs. One of the most important of these needs is to preserve meaningful connections to the past.

Despite his tireless efforts to find Inuit communities living in a primitive state, Rasmussen was quite willing to use modern tools himself without believing that he was compromising cultural identity. On the Fifth Thule Expedition, he travelled with a gramophone and recordings that he used to entertain the Inuit groups he encountered. The most popular recording that he played for his hosts was the recent hit, "Alexander's Ragtime Band." He regretted not being able to film an Inuit song festival.

> The emotional atmosphere in a *qagse* (song festival house) among men and women enlivened by song is something that cannot be conveyed save by actual experience. Some slight idea of it may perhaps be given some day, when the "talking film" has attained a higher degree of technical perfection—if it gets there in time it would then have to be by a combination of the songs in the Eskimo tongue and the dancing in living pictures. Unfortunately, I was unable to record their melodies on the phonograph as our instrument was out of order.

The emotional intensity of the song festivals was also commented on by Peter Freuchen. "The whole audience is possessed by the song and emotions are whipped up to a frightening pitch. Realizing this, the artist must always end his song with something to make his audience laugh." In 1955, a song festival was held by the small group of Caribou Eskimo at Ennadai Lake to honour their visitor Geert van den Steenhoven. He felt privileged to observe what he considered to be the "purest of Eskimo dancing and singing" performed by this very remote people. After several hours, they concluded their performance with a special treat for the visitor. The men formed a circle and walked in a ring with backs slightly bent, humming a rhythmic melody. Only after a time did van den Steenhoven realize that they were imitating an Indian drum dance and the tune they were humming was "Summertime" from *Porgy and Bess*.

Diamond Jenness was able to make phonograph recordings of several shamanic performances among the Copper Eskimo although his first attempt was disappointing. The angakoq Ilatsiak had seen Jenness record several songs and asked to speak into the machine under the inspiration of his familiar spirit Kingaudlik.

> [Ilatsiak] was rather short of stature, so we had to raise him on a box to bring his face level with the horn; perched on this box he protruded his face into the bell of the horn and nervously kicked his legs out behind him, one after the other, in the manner of a person skipping over a rope. The usual preliminaries of a shamanistic

performance were omitted; he merely paused a moment to collect his wits (or to give his familiar time to enter him), then said what he had to say and stood down. Some of the words are scarcely audible in the record owing to his jumping. As usual too, it is difficult to attach any meaning to them, but the literal interpretation of this first oracle was, "Where? Give me liver, liver, it is excellent. I hear speech" — a remark that Ilatsiak's adopted son understood to mean that his father's familiar Kingaudlik was asking for some liver.

Some subsequent recordings were more comprehensible, partly due to Ilatsiak's wife, who was also an angakoq. Evoking an image recognizable in many cultures, she can be heard in the background urging her husband or his helping spirit to speak more clearly.

A few years later, Rasmussen observed Netsit, the adopted son of Ilatsiak, climb to the summit of a steep, black rock island to offer a cigarette and some matches at the grave of his father. "Netsit thought that the gift of so great a luxury as a cigarette would surely have the power to call up the soul of the dead man, and secure his protection for us against the troublesome weather we were having." At the same time, he recited a magic song to the memory of his father.

> Big Man, big Man
> Make smooth your big hands
> And your big feet,
> Make them swift running
> And look far ahead.
> Big Man, big Man,
> Smooth out your thoughts
> And look far ahead.
> Big Man, big Man
> Let fall your weapon now.

Ilatsiak's spirit must have been pleased by the song and the unusual offering. The weather was much improved the next day.

Throughout the historical period, the Inuit have shown a great willingness to accept new products and technologies from phonographs to cigarettes and adapt them to old purposes. A Copper Eskimo hunter who had lost his rifle asked Jenness to use his compass and tell him where to find it. In the early 1950s in Pond Inlet, Idlouk was delighted with the walky-talky used by Katherine Scherman. Within minutes he was devising plans to revolutionize seal hunting. When Peter Pitseolak returned to Cape Dorset in 1946 after a lengthy stay in a southern hospital, he acquired the first radio in the region and used it to listen to the national weather forecasts from Winnipeg. Very soon, there was a rumour that he had become an angakoq during his time in the south since he could now predict the weather. This culture trait is very evident in Georgia's description of the development of Igloolik Community Radio since it went on the air in 1976. "Not only do Inuit of all ages talk over the air from the four year old wishing his brother a happy birthday to the elders telling tales of the old days . . . but an amazing percentage of the population also mans the controls. When they lived in camps, Inuit not only told the stories that are their history, but they wove the happenings of the day into scary, thrilling or humorous vignettes. Now they either broadcast the stories live or put them on cassettes."

Georgia's very personal diary of arctic life emphasizes the continuity of Inuit behaviour and beliefs. This persistence of values represents no small achievement in the midst of plane and helicopter landings and a continuous stream of outsiders through the transient centres. In her account, she describes the continuing importance of storytelling not only on the radio but in more traditional forms. One Repulse Bay storyteller particularly impressed her. "I had been able to catch what he was saying long before I had learned enough Inuktitut to understand anyone else because he expressed himself not only with his voice, but with every muscle of his body. Face working, hands fluttering, arms flailing, body twisting, he could talk for hours without respite. Among a people renowned for storytelling, Oqak was legendary."

Writing about the acceptance of Christianity, Georgia's description echoes the pragmatic attitudes observed by Mathiassen and Freuchen in the same area two generations before. "With Christian baptism, the Inuit acquired one more name and spirit, quite acceptable to a people glad of yet another spiritual protector. When the children go to school, perhaps to be enrolled under their Christian names, they usually maintain their name-spirit identity outside of school, in their families and in the total Inuit society." Peter Pitseolak remembered that when he was growing up in Cape Dorset people changed their names frequently and the introduction of Christianity gave them a new source of names. "When we started to be able to read the Bible, people would pick names from the Bible and say, 'Maybe if I have this name, God will save me.' If people could not read the Bible, someone who could would pick a name for them. It didn't always have to be Mosessee. They'd pick names that were related to the Bible. There was Kumwartok — 'going up', Kaka — 'hills', Gotilliaktuk — 'going to God.'"

In the early years of this century, Vilhjalmur Stefansson witnessed the rapid spread of Christianity among the Inuit of northern Alaska and the Mackenzie River area. He was skeptical of the common belief of the converts that their lives had been transformed almost completely when they accepted the new religion. His observations led him to conclude that the new beliefs were simply superimposed on the old ways. One time, the young guide Ilavinirk argued with him that Christianity had produced great changes; "The people of Kotzebue Sound were formerly very bad, but they are all good now. In my father's time and when I was young they used to lie and to steal and to work on Sunday." Stefansson replied, "But don't they, as a matter of fact, tell lies now occasionally?" Ilavinirk had to admit, "Oh, yes, they sometimes do." "Well, don't they really, as a matter of fact, tell as many lies as they ever did?" "Well, yes, perhaps they do." "And don't they, as a matter of fact, steal about as frequently as ever?" "Well, possibly. But they don't work on Sunday."

7. I Don't Forget My Old Way

THE PROBLEM of taking from the past what remains valid in the present is not unique to the Inuit but is common to all cultures in the last years of the twentieth century. Perhaps the central problem of our time is the loss of values under the influence of scientific inquiry and relative morality. We are all engaged in the difficult task of reviving meaning in outmoded and incomplete models of reality. For the Inuit, this problem of cultural meaning has been posed in an acute form, to make the transition from a stone age hunting culture in a few generations or even in one lifetime. It may be that the Inuit have some advantages over other cultures since they have no rigid ideology to prevent them from accepting useful innovations. In fact, they are following their own cultural values in doing this.

Traditions are more adaptable than is commonly believed. By the 1920s, the Netsilik people had abandoned their old belief that someone who cut his hair also cut away part of his soul. They remembered the tradition, but no one paid any attention to it. In 1910, as reported by Diamond Jenness, the Copper Eskimo learned from the people living to the west that, if they did not cut off a fragment from every skin they sold to the fur traders, "the animals would follow the skins and leave the country also." This seemed reasonable since it helped explain the disappearance of caribou from parts of Alaska and the Mackenzie River delta. A new custom or taboo was introduced. The Copper Eskimo culture observed by Jenness in the 1910s was in a state of rapid transition caused not only by the influence of traders and missionaries but also by the competing customs of Inuit groups living to the west and east. A few years earlier, Franz Boas reported that some new customs had been introduced recently in the Repulse Bay area "on account of the immigration of some people from Ponds Bay [Pond Inlet] who claimed that the customs of the Aivilik were wrong." This experience was repeated in the same area in 1922 when the two fugitives from Pond Inlet converted the Aivilik to a form of Christianity. Among the Caribou Eskimo, Igjugarjuk tolerantly told his visitors from Greenland and Denmark, "No one will be offended if you do not understand our food; we all have our different customs."

Like all other peoples, the Inuit have tried to fit their new experiences into the framework of their old customs and beliefs. In all areas of the north, the story is told that some older Inuit were not impressed by the flights of men to the moon beginning in 1969, since in the old days this had been a common feat of the powerful angakoqs. The early explorers were commonly thought to have come from the moon. In some regions, the manager of the Hudson's Bay Company trading post assumed many of the functions of the isumatok (leader), while the Anglican or Catholic missionary played the role of the angakoq. In recent times, the Pentecostal movement has displaced the more restrained

145. Anonymous   Dorset Culture c. 1000 A.D.
Harpoon Head
A harpoon head with incised lines showing a primitive face. It is conjectured that these objects were used as amulets believed to have the power to guide the harpoon to the animal.

146. Anonymous   Spence Bay c. 1975   *Harpoon Head*
An archaic carving that recalls the spiritual significance of the hunt, a harpoon tip is transformed into an image of flight. The helping spirit of the hunter guided the harpoon to its target.

147. Thomas Sivuraq
Baker Lake 1989 *Transformation*
"The way is made ready for me, the
way is opening before me." With
walrus tusks, ears of a bear and wings
about to open, the angakoq displays
his mastery of the elements as he
leaves on a spirit journey.

Anglican and Catholic religions in some communities. The dynamic interactive
services of the Pentecostal churches resemble more closely the participatory
angakoq performances of the traditional culture. Some members of these funda-
mentalist churches are inspired to talk in tongues, believing that this is a manifes-
tation of unseen forces.

The anthropologist Jean Briggs lived for seventeen months in 1963-64 as the
adoptive daughter of Inuttiaq, an Anglican lay preacher of the
Utkuhikhalingmiut (the "Dwellers in the Land of Soapstone" — a small group of
Caribou Eskimo living in the Back River area between Baker Lake and Gjoa
Haven). Her initial goal was to study shamanism, but she found that the group
had become devout Anglicans who refused to discuss their traditional beliefs.

They told her that their angakoqs were either in hiding or in hell. One time Inuttiaq lectured Briggs on the nature of his authority as a religious leader. His conception of his role was strongly reminiscent of earlier ways.

> Nakliguhuktuq (the Anglican deacon in Gjoa Haven) had appointed him king over the Utku, he told me; the deacon had told him that if people resisted his, Inuttiaq's, religious teachings, then Inuttiaq should write to him and he would come quickly and scold the disbelievers. Moreover, Inuttiaq added, "If people don't want to believe Nakliguhuktuq either, then Nakliguhuktuq will write to Cambridge Bay, and a bigger leader, the *kapluna* (white man) king in Cambridge Bay, will come in an airplane with a big and well-made whip and will whip people. It will hurt a great deal."

One of Inuttiaq's predecessors as lay preacher had attempted to exaggerate his importance by claiming that he made journeys into the sky to talk to God. He warned the Utku that a very black man would come and eat them if they continued their pagan ways. When they could find no precedent for this in their Bibles, they wrote to the kapluna missionary in Spence Bay for confirmation.

The majority of the Back River people were settled in Baker Lake beginning in the late 1950s. In Rasmussen's account, their difficult existence on the land had been made bearable by their celebration of life in their songs and stories. At the time they were resettled, they were among the most impoverished of all Inuit groups. Totally dependent on caribou hunting, they faced starvation when the caribou herds diminished in size and changed their migration routes. In the early 1970s, K. J. Butler described their difficult adjustment to a settled life.

> The Back River are the people who came from the wrong side of the mountain, literally. There's a ridge on the side of the Back River—nobody crossed that. They were outcasts. They're the most recent into the settlement and for the most part, therefore, the least acculturated. Interestingly, they constitute the majority of our artists. For a people who supposedly no longer practice or have anything to do with shamanism, it is curious that their art appears to be predominantly about shamanic subjects.

When Rasmussen visited the Utkuhikhalingmiut in 1923, he estimated their population to be 164 souls. They made a very favourable impression as "the handsomest and most hospitable as well as the most cultured people of all those I met with throughout my journey; and the cleanest and most contented to boot." Two generations later as observed by Butler, they were the "least acculturated" group in Baker Lake.

No white men had ever settled among the Utku as a result, they believed, of a spell cast in 1833 when the first outsiders had passed through their land. After they left, an angakoq said that they would bring no good and uttered a spell to prevent them from ever returning. This spell proved to be almost completely effective over the next hundred years. Old Ikinilik belonged to this small group of Caribou Eskimo. When Rasmussen asked him, "What do you understand by 'the soul'?", he was surprised by the question but answered, "It is something beyond understanding, that which makes me a human being." However,

**148. Simon Tookoome
Baker Lake 1991** *Inukshuk*
**The form on the top of the carving
represents an inukshuk, a pile of
stones used as a landmark when
travelling. Caribou and muskox
are frightened by the inukshuks.**

Ikinilik's imagination failed him when Rasmussen attempted to explain that his words would be made known to many people by means of the "talk-marks" recorded in his notebooks. These marks would be printed on sheets of fine "skin" for men to learn what was happening each day. Ikinilik enjoyed this as a humorous exaggeration, saying that "the world of the white men was big, no doubt, yet it could not after all be bigger than that a man might learn all the news there was by enquiring at the nearest tent."

In an enigmatic sculpture, Peter Airo of Payne Bay in Arctic Quebec recalls some of his earliest memories from childhood. The explanation that he gives of his carving illustrates in personal terms the universal problem of adapting old models to new situations. This account is taken directly from an oral telling by the artist.

I was born on September 13, 1933. My name is Peter Airo. In 1939 I was starting to hear about airplanes, but I felt that I had seen them in my mind from the stories

149. Peter Airo   Kangirsuk 1978   *Airplane*
"In 1939 [when I was five or six years old], I was starting to hear about airplanes, but I
felt that I had seen them in my mind from the stories I had heard. That's why the carving
looks like what I thought airplanes looked like."

I had heard. That's why the carving looks like what I thought airplanes looked like. Also I had heard that there were policemen but I hadn't seen any. Also, I had heard about soldiers but I hadn't seen any.

I used to be really serious and frightened when I heard about soldiers and policemen. That's why I set this up with a policeman and a soldier the way I imagined them. There are police and soldiers in the plane the way I imagined them years ago.

I used to hear that the policeman had a dog and was always holding his dog. I used to hear that the policeman's dog might get me when I was bad — that's what my parents told me. So I used to be a good boy for my parents.

I used to hear about soldiers. I used to think that a soldier always held onto his gun. I also used to think that soldiers might come over and shoot me if I was bad. I used to try to imagine how they looked before I saw them. And I thought that an airplane doesn't fly, I thought that airplanes were on the ground, or on the water. And I thought that airplanes would have a kayak too, because I thought that kayaks were the only transportation on the water. Even today I would like to be a pilot myself, because I know everything about airplanes now, but I don't forget my old way of thinking and my old way of life.

In telling this story, Peter Airo uses a tentative repetitive style that recalls the conventions of traditional storytelling. He reminds us of the difficulties that all children experience in constructing visual images of reality. Peter's concerns expressed in this account are probably related to the outbreak of war in 1939 when there was a substantial increase in government activity in the north. Somewhat predictably, his parents used the threat of the policeman's dog to

150. Josiah Nuilaalik   Baker Lake 1991   *Dog Spirit*
If they were not good, small children were told that Sedna's dog husband would come and take them away.

frighten their young son into good behaviour. A generation earlier it would have been Sedna's dog that punished any transgression of the rules. In northern communities, the policeman was often called *amakro* (the wolf) for his habit of lurking in the background, constantly watching for any mistakes. Robert Williamson observed that a common threat used by Rankin Inlet parents with young children was, "If you are not good, the Government man will get you." We can only speculate that in an earlier time the ambition to learn to fly would have taken a very different form.

In the traditional life, the angakoqs had the ability to see into the spirit world and, equally important, the ability to convince others of the reality and signifi-

151. Anonymous   Repulse Bay c.1965
Concentration
An unknown artist has captured the angakoq's struggle to see into the hidden world. The shaman sees through darkness to find the causes of events in the past and future.

152. Barnabus Arnasungaaq
Baker Lake 1992   *Muskox Shaman*
Calling on her muskox helping spirit, an angakoq enters the shamanic state and prepares for the soul journey.

cance of their dreams and visions. On occasion, these powers survived the conversion to Christianity. Peter Freuchen recorded a very unusual instance in the Igloolik region.

> Aua told us that only last summer he had had a remarkable experience which might have been more remarkable if it had not been for a little girl who laughed at the wrong time. He was sitting outside his tent carving a walrus tusk when he saw three men approaching the settlement. He did not know who they might be, but suddenly recognized them as the new gods of the Trinity, the Father, the Son and the Holy Ghost. Aua shouted for everyone to come out and receive the dignified guests. And then, when a certain little girl discovered they wore pants of rabbit skin and very tall caps, she had to laugh. This made the Trinity angry, and, while they smiled forgivingly, they altered their course so they passed by without stopping or even speaking a word in greeting. The natives had been greatly disappointed, but they said the Holy Ghost presented such a laughable aspect from the rear that they all gave way to their mirth. His posteriors curved in instead of out.

One interpretation of this experience is that Aua and the others were attempting to call forth the helping spirits of the Christian religion. They were not successful since some skepticism remained about the new beliefs. Earlier in his life, Aua had had similar experiences. Promised as an angakoq from before birth, a strict discipline was imposed on him during his childhood and early youth. Despite all the preparations, his efforts to become an angakoq by the ordinary methods were not successful. Famous angakoqs were consulted and given gifts with no results. Finally, as Rasmussen describes, "At last, without knowing how, he perceived that a change had come over him, a great glow of intense light pervaded all his being . . . and a feeling of inexpressible joy came over him, and he burst into a song."

Aua was a transitional figure who personified the many changes taking place in Inuit life. Twenty years before, he had worked for Captain Comer, the famous American whaling captain who was called Angakoq because of his photography and his other powers. Rasmussen had visited Aua's camp in 1922 before they had been converted to Christianity by the missionaries from Pond Inlet. When he returned a year later, he observed from a distance the little white flags above every igloo.

> As I drove up, men, women and children trooped out and formed up in line outside Aua's hut, and as soon as I had reined in my team, the whole party began singing a hymn. The tune was so unlike what they were accustomed to in their own pagan chants that they bungled it a little, but there was no mistaking the earnestness and pious feeling which inspired it. There was something very touching in such a greeting; these poor folks had plainly found in the new faith a refuge that meant a great deal in their lives.

The year before, they had greeted him by leaping around in an outburst of high spirits while now he was greeted by a solemn ceremony. However, the formality wore off quickly and, before long, "the old easy merriment showed forth again." Aua was soon describing the old beliefs as if nothing had changed.

Franz Boas recorded Comer's account of how he had come very close to ruining Aua's earnest efforts to become a shaman.

In the winter of 1901-1902 a young man was trying to become an angakoq, but had not been able to secure a guardian spirit. One day Captain Comer happened to be in the young man's house, and, slapping him on the back, asked him how he was getting on. Then the other angakut declared that by this slap whatever progress he had made had been driven out, and the young man would have to begin all over again. After a few days the men led the young novice to the vessel, walking Indian file, swinging their arms and chanting a song. Captain Comer was requested to tie a piece of new cloth to a strap which the novice wore over one shoulder, to throw up his hands, and to say "Enough!" which would drive away the evil effects of having touched the novice.

This complex incident indicates the acceptance of Comer's powers as an angakoq, probably after a few days of furious debate. To conclude a seance, the shamans would say *taima*, *taima*, "Enough, enough!" Another time after a very successful whaling season, a woman gave Comer a new pair of boots and asked him to do something so that her son would become a good hunter and not be lazy. "Not knowing what was best to give, I asked some of the older natives. They told me to give her a lock of grey hair from each temple, also a small piece from each wristband of my shirt, which I did, and she was more than pleased."

Captain Comer also gave a detailed description of his friend's initiation as an angakoq when Aua finally received his helping spirits.

One day when he was caribou hunting near the peninsula Amitoq, he killed three caribou. On the following day he saw four large bucks, one of which was very fat. He struck it with an arrow, and the caribou began to run to and fro. Its antlers and its skin dropped off, its head became smaller, and soon it assumed the form of a woman with finely made clothes. Soon she fell down, giving birth to a boy, and then she died. The other caribou had turned into men, who told him to cover the woman and the child with moss, so that nobody should find them. They told him to straighten out her body; but he was only able to move one arm, because she was exceedingly heavy. After he had covered up the bodies, the men told him to return to his people to tell them what had happened, and to have his clothing made in the same way as that of the woman.

As Comer recorded this story, his paper rested on a woman's shoulders. Aua objected, believing that his helping spirit would not like to have a woman touched by the paper on which so important a story was written. The angakoq coat that he made following the instructions of the caribou-men had animal figures on the shoulders representing "children of the earth." On the front of the coat, two hands outlined in white skin were intended to ward off evil spirits. The angakoq's hands symbolized his human identity in his confrontations with the spirits. Captain Comer remarked that the novice angakoq had not yet proved his powers. Some of his claims were received very skeptically by the others. However, while Aua was telling his story, Comer noticed that "the women who were near covered their heads with their hoods, for fear of the angakoq's protecting spirit."

Another transitional figure described by Rasmussen was a young leader of the Utkuhikhalingmiut, the group that made the most favourable impression on him in his travels.

A young man, tall and broad-shouldered, a head higher than all the others, was at first the one who acted as spokesman for his fellow villagers. And he did so with the dignity of a chieftain.

As soon as the arrival formalities were over and they understood that we were friends, he informed me that four big salmon caches, deposited last summer, had just been opened, and that I had only to let my dogs loose when they were to be fed. . . . When our tent was up he came again to me and asked my name. He himself was called Uunaimitauq, the warmer. The introduction proceeded under due observance of the dignity that the villagers had displayed from the very moment of our arrival, and with his eyes steadfastly fixed on mine he questioned me: "Tell me, are you a white man of the kind who forbid Eskimos to come into their tents?"

I answered that while there it was my object to learn as much as possible in the shortest possible time and that anyone who could visit me in my tent was welcome.

Uunaimitauq need not have been concerned about this visitor. Rasmussen was a firm believer of the Inuit saying that a tent is not full until it bursts. It was in this small community that old Ikinilik claimed that they had lived themselves out of their old customs. But he also reassured the visitors about the safety of their possessions. He told them, "Among our people, it is only dogs who steal."

Four decades later in 1966, Eugene Arima interviewed the old hunter Anguhalluq, who had recently settled in Baker Lake. "He was very tall and good looking, with a shock of grey hair wildly radiating about his handsome features. . . . Later we got to talk and the first thing he said was that he was not Anguhalluq or Young Bull Caribou. People just called him that, he said. He was really Uunaimitaaq. His honest forthrightness was thus salient from the start, and it was evident that he had always been that way." In the following years until he lost his breath in 1982, Anguhalluq (Anguhudlaq, Angosaglo) became famous for his drawings of scenes from traditional life. He was always consulted as the authority on the Back River versions of the old stories. His last years in Baker Lake were spent quietly but, as Arima describes, "at times he would smile and suddenly be again that bold young man of long ago, eyes sparkling through all the weathering of endless days outdoors. Active, he would still walk out when it was fine weather, slowly but steadily, over the low hills of Baker, a .22 rifle hung across his back."

Among the many artists at Povungnituk, Joe Talirunili was described as one of the real old-timers. Johnny Pov, one of his contemporaries, recollected that "Joe always competed in being a man. . . . He hunted whenever he could and he shared his food with others. As long as he had food in his house, he shared it with everyone." Born in 1899 (or 1906 according to another account), he could remember a time when there were no rifles. In his later years, he recalled his surprise as a child when he first saw the white people's matches. As a young man, he worked for a time with some prospectors and learned of some new possibilities. "It was during this time that I became aware that it was possible to write things and to communicate on paper and that things would be written here and the same things would reach to the white man's land." One generation before, his father worked for three months with another group of prospectors, but he was slower to understand the new ways. When he returned to his home, he was asked if he had been given anything. He replied that all he received was some pieces of paper, but he did not know what they were for and he threw them away. In an exasperated tone, Joe commented, "That was in the days when we knew practically nothing."

Until his death in 1976, Joe Talirunili told and retold in many sculptures and drawings the story of a perilous migration that he had experienced in his youth.

> Once, when we were crossing from an island in Hudson's Bay to the mainland, we had many problems. We had nothing to sit on when we were making our boat except the snow. When we slept, we would lie in the snow and then, because it was spring, when we awakened the sun would have melted the snow under us and we would be lying in water. At that time, my father was badly crippled in one of his legs. He had left the ice in a hurry but had forgotten his rifle.
>
> Once we had our boat fixed, we tried to cross. My grandmother, who was with us, had been elected as the leader of the boat. She wanted to pray. She said, in these words, "God is the one who wants to hear things. If we pray, he will therefore listen to what we want to say." And when she was saying this, the ice was fighting with each other—the big chunks were fighting with the small pieces of ice.
>
> Then there was a great crash of thunder which frightened all of the children in the boat and made us cover our ears with our hands, it was so loud. And when the thunder stopped, we could see that a path had been made through the ice for us and in this path there was just flat water with no pieces of ice. This led us to the land.
>
> My grandmother then said, "Since God has listened to us, let us try to reach the land with our boat." When we approached the land, although we were moving, it seemed like the land was moving away from us and my grandmother said, "The land is moving away from us and leaving us behind."
>
> My father's brother, whose name was Amitok, meaning "the thin one" said, "Let us shoot at the land. Since we have one gun with us, let us shoot at the land." He shot at the land and although it was a long way away, we could see that his bullet had hit the side of a mountain. Then it seemed as if we moved forward quickly and in a very short time we were up to the land.
>
> We landed in a place that was very steep. We had to take a rope and when we got to the shore, we secured the boat to the shore with this rope. During that time, for almost a week, the wind blew very hard and we could not move from where we were. That was the time my mother said that we might be having to eat each other because we were so hungry. The weather changed at last and when the ice slackened off, we went to find some people.

In this telling of the story, we can detect an uneasy balance of modern and ancient concepts. At one level, it describes an actual migration of people at the limits of endurance. Several months of arduous effort had been necessary to gather the skins and other materials needed to construct their sealskin boat. At another level, it is an account of a spiritual journey. The prayer that opens the path through the ice recalls the shaman's cry, "The way is made ready for me, the way is opening before me," as he begins his journey to the spirit world.

The new belief in Christianity gave a powerful focus to the anxieties of this small group of about forty people and seemed to point the way forward.

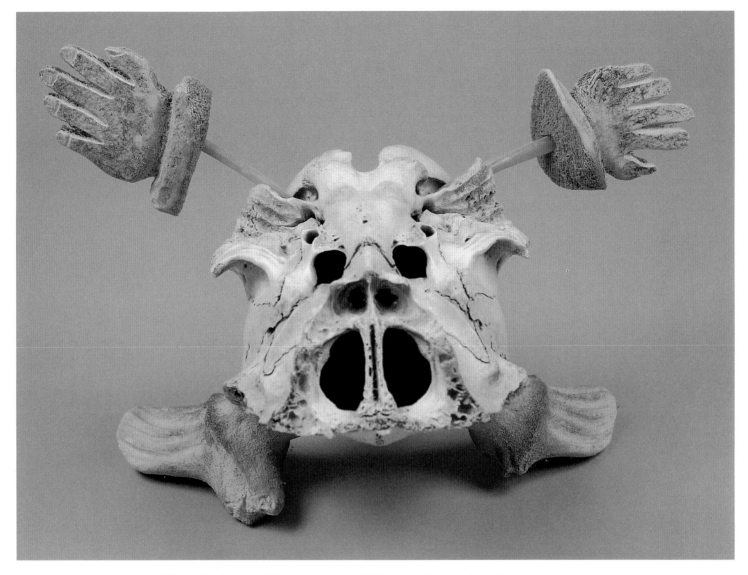

153. Manasie Akpaliapik   Arctic Bay 1988   *Sculpin Helping Spirit*
The sculpin is a bony fish with very little meat that the people eat when there is no other food. Manasie says that the people of Arctic Bay think of the sculpin as a helping spirit in times of need.

However, the threat of starvation would justify a return to older ways of behaviour. The incident with the rifle is very revealing. Evidently the land was bewitched and would not allow the migrating people to approach. They were attempting to reach the Ottawa Islands, the mysterious land of Arvilik where the Lumak legend was believed to have taken place. By accepting the new religion, the people were afraid that they had offended the spirits. This problem is resolved when Amitok has the courage to defy the malevolent spirits of the land with the more powerful magic of the rifle. Joe's account ends with their desire to reestablish contact with the human world. When they did find some people at last, the grandmother called out to them, "We are not the liced ones [Indians]. We are only Inuit."

More than one hundred years ago, Lucien Turner recorded a legend that also deals with the changes taking place in Inuit life. By adapting a familiar story, it attempts to explain the coming of the white people in terms of old concepts.

As in Talirunili's story, extreme hardships prepared the Inuit to anticipate and accept changes in their way of life.

> The Eskimo were on the verge of starvation and had eaten nearly all their food. They saw that in a few more days death would come. The greatest Tungaksoak (angakoq) or great Tungak determined to bring relief and prophesied that people having light hair and white skins would come in an immense umiak (sealskin boat). He placed a young puppy on a chip and another on an old sealskin boot, and set them adrift on the water. The puppies drifted in different directions, and in the course of time the one on the chip returned and brought with it the Indians. A long time after that, when the people had nearly forgotten the other puppy, a strange white object like an iceberg came directly toward the shore. In a few minutes the puppy, now a man, announced that the people had come with many curious things in their vessel. The man immediately became a dog.

154. Mary Inutiq Illauq Clyde River 1968 *Dog Child*
Sedna's dog children, half human and half dog, became the ancestors of the Indians and the white men.

155. Jimmy Nookiguak   Broughton Island 1975   *Dog Child*
"She made a boat for the young dogs, setting up two sticks for masts in the soles of her boots, and sent the puppies across the ocean....They arrived in the land beyond the sea and became the ancestors of the Europeans."

156. David Ruben Piqtoukun   Paulatuk, Toronto 1991
Dog Children
The dog children with white eyes will become the ancestors of the white men. Those with red eyes will give rise to the Indians. The artist explained that different people see things in different ways.

In Turner's very incomplete story, there is an obvious preoccupation to extend the concepts of Inuit mythology in order to describe and explain the new influences. Among the Aivilik Eskimo, the shamanic word for a white man was *taujaq*, "an almost human being." After Diamond Jenness had lived with the Copper Eskimo for more than a year, he was surprised when his guide Higilak announced as a great discovery one day that the white men were no different from the Eskimos.

Forty years after Turner, Rasmussen heard almost the same story from Igjugarjuk but he was already familiar with the legend as it was told in Greenland. In Igjugarjuk's version, a girl who marries a dog commands her children who will become Indians: "Take vengeance for all the wrong your grandfather did to me, and show yourselves henceforward thirsty for blood as often as you meet one of the Inuit." To her dog children who will become the white men, she commands: "Go out into the world and become skilful in all manner of work!" This last command was obeyed only too well. Igjugarjuk's first wife Kivkarjuk adapted the famous story to give an ingenious explanation for the inventiveness of the foreigners. In her account, the boat carrying Sedna's dog children who became the white men began to take on water. To save themselves, they had to work very hard as they sailed over the sea. Kivkarjuk concluded that this was the reason that the white men are "always in a hurry and have much to do and are clever at all kinds of work with their hands."

Among all artists of the modern period, Davidialuk has a special place for his single-minded effort to document and preserve the past through the new art forms. He was the son of Amitok who said "Let us shoot at the land" in the migration journey described by Joe Talirunili. In a 1975 Povungnituk print, Davidialuk depicts his father raising his rifle to shoot at the land. The presence of

157. Tukiki Manomie   Cape Dorset c. 1980   *Sea Spirit*
"[My brother] Pootoogook also saw something once — he didn't know exactly what. He saw it from a distance when I was young. Maybe it was Talilayu [Sedna]. He thought he'd seen a seal but when he got close he saw arms waving. That was no seal" (Peter Pitseolak in Eber 1975, 95).

the spirits is suggested by vivid stars and northern lights crossing the sky. In his retelling of the legend of Lumak, Davidialuk may have described his own motivation for telling stories; "his descendants wanted to keep this story alive." Since self-assertion was not highly valued in traditional life, this motivation is stated in impersonal terms. Following the values of a different culture, another documentary artist, Robert Flaherty, expressed his similar aim more directly, "I wanted to tell others about them."

Davidialuk's life can be seen as emblematic of the development of the Inuit in this century. Born in 1910 to a nomadic life that depended on hunting for survival, he died in 1976 on an airplane while being sent south for emergency medical treatment. He had a reputation as a poor hunter and his life was one of hardship and privation until his later years when his artistic ability was recognized. The period of his greatest creative activity followed a lengthy stay in a tuberculosis hospital in Hamilton, Ontario, in the late 1960s. One story that he returned to many times in sculptures, drawings and prints is the legend of the hunter who encounters a mermaid. He claimed that "many people had seen fish-men and fish-women when they were hunting sea animals and they feared these creatures." In this written version, he gives the story a very unusual ending.

A poor man was gathering driftwood along the shoreline when he caught sight of an arm lying on the beach. He thought it was probably a human in need of help but, all the same, as he approached the arm, he felt some regret at not having a weapon. As he drew near, he saw that the arm belonged to a creature who was half human and half fish. The torso was that of a woman with long braided hair. And she was huge—almost three times the size of the inuk. But she spoke the Inuit language saying, "Please help me. I have to reach the water but am unable to go any further."

The hunter replied, "But you are so big. I couldn't lift you if I wanted to." The mermaid answered, "I see you are carrying a bundle of sticks. Take one and use it to roll me towards the water. But I warn you. Do not touch me with your hands. If you do, they will stick to me forever."

The hunter did as she suggested, being careful not to touch her. Just before she reached the water, the mermaid asked him what reward he would like for helping her. The hunter did not reply, however, as he could not think of anything he wanted from under the water. The mermaid persisted saying, "Please name those things you have wanted all your life." Still the man did not answer. There was nothing he wanted from the mermaid. But to show her gratitude, she said, "I will leave a record player, a rifle and a sewing machine here on this spot for you to pick up tomorrow."

Filled with disbelief, but curious, the hunter returned the next morning. He was astonished to see the three gifts she had promised—a record player, a rifle and a sewing machine. Everyone visited him to see the three wonders and, eventually, people were able to copy them and make more. That's how these things came to exist and that is the end of the story.

In this remarkable story, Davidialuk describes a modern encounter of the human and spirit worlds, the great theme of the narrative tradition. Like all contemporary Inuit, Sedna is out of her natural element and needs human help to return.

158. Davidialuk Alasua Amittu   Povungnituk 1976   *Three Gifts*
He was astonished to see the three gifts that she had promised — a record player, a rifle
and a sewing machine. Everyone visited him to see the three wonders, and, eventually,
people were able to copy them and make more.

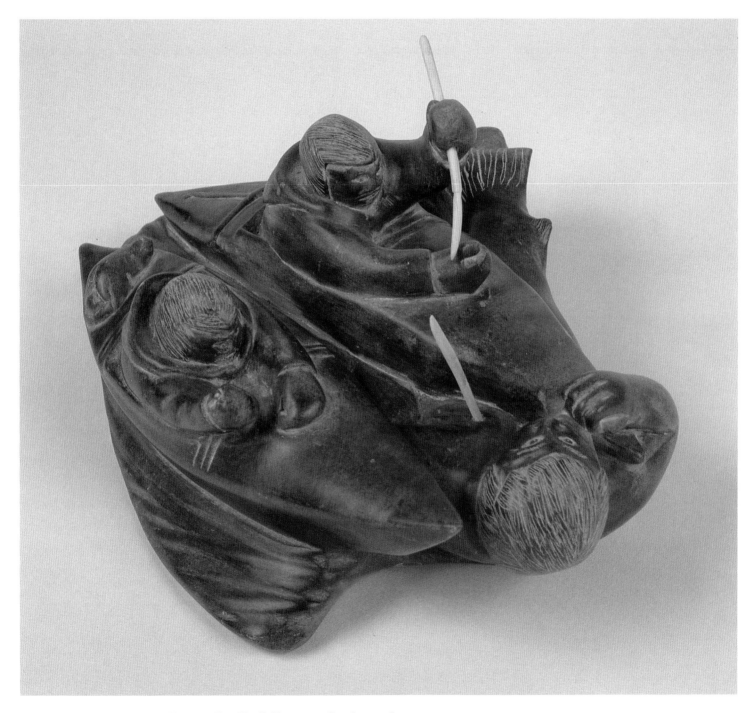

159. Nowyapik   Akulivik 1978   *Confrontation*
The magic words and songs of the hunters seeking seals and walrus may work too well.
The mother of the sea animals herself may rise from her unhappy home, attempting to
rejoin the human world. Sedna must be forced to return to the bottom of the sea to live in
the world of the imagination.

160. Manasie Akpaliapik Arctic Bay 1988 *Sedna and Dog Child*
A pensive, calm Sedna whose mood is indicated by her graceful pose and the beautiful
braid.

Following the old taboos, the woman with long braided hair is not called by her name. It may be that the hunter no longer recognizes her and has forgotten her name, but she does belong to the people since she speaks their language. Very significantly, the encounter occurs on the shore, the traditional visualization of the boundary between the human and spirit domains. It is not mediated by an angakoq but is a direct confrontation of the hunter and the powerful spirit. The poor man wishes he had a weapon yet does not call on the protection of amulets or magic words. According to Davidialuk, Sedna's powers do continue to exist but in a very different way. The storyteller adapts and extends the ancient creation myth to account for the three miraculous inventions. With modifications, the old system of beliefs is still able to explain the modern world of the Inuit. The carefully chosen gifts that Sedna brings can be seen as symbolic of the many changes in Inuit life. The rifle symbolizes the new activities of men, the sewing machine refers to the domain of women, and the record player represents the continuing importance of songs and stories.

An event very similar to the story of the hunter and the mermaid occurred in Davidialuk's own life. Along with George Swinton, he was invited to attend the opening of the Sculpture Inuit exhibition at the Danish National Museum in Copenhagen in 1972. He spent one week exploring the city, fascinated by the strange sights. In the National Museum, he saw on display the many thousands of ethnological artifacts collected during the Fifth Thule Expedition, among them Kinalik's angakoq belt and the clothes of a Netsilik boy weighed down with eighty amulets. Seeing these objects, Davidialuk must have been reminded of the life he had known in his youth. No other person will ever see them again in the same way. During his stay in Denmark, he may have seen the large granite statue of Knud Rasmussen facing the sea near Copenhagen. On this monument, there is an inscription based on an Inuit song that celebrates the endless journey of life.

> Only the Air Spirits know
> What I shall find beyond the mountains
> Yet I urge my sledge team on
> Drive on and on
> On and on!

Like every visitor to Copenhagen, one of the sights that Davidialuk would have seen is the famous statue on the harbour shore of the little mermaid of another storyteller, Hans Christian Andersen. After his initial surprise and perhaps a moment of fear, we can imagine that he felt a strong impulse to help the half-woman, half-fish creature return to the sea.

8. Odark's Journey

THE INFLUENCE of the outside world was inevitably to become so over-whelming that it defied all attempts to incorporate it in the ancient frame-work of stories and beliefs. The most dramatic illustration is without doubt the construction of the Thule airbase by 7500 American servicemen and workers in the summer of 1951. Their construction site was in the very centre of the tradi-tional summer gathering place for the Polar Eskimos. They called this region Arnaluap Nuna, the land of the young woman who would not have a husband and became the mother of the sea creatures. More than 3000 Americans spent the following winter at the new base, ten times the Polar Eskimo population. The base radio station KOLD soon became the strongest signal in the Arctic, a modern version of the Great Spirit of the Air.

The French anthropologist Jean Malaurie was present to record the halting reactions of one old man to this invasion.

> "Thousands and thousands of Americans," Uutaaq said in his hoarse voice. "Amerlaqaat, you lose track of how many. They come down from the sky every day. There's the atomic bomb, too. . . . We've been here a thousand years, we Inuit. We always thought Thule was an important place on earth. . . . After all, we were the ones who discovered it. . . . Thule . . . The Inuit also say that they're going to heat the ice field and make it melt; that way there will hardly be winter anymore. . . . Then they're going to send us to the North Pole. That's why Piulissuaq spent fifteen years trying to go there with the Inuit. . . . Ah! we under-stand everything now. . . ."

Half a century before in 1902, Rasmussen had recorded a literal account given by Uutaaq (otherwise known as Odark or Otaq or Oodaaq or Oo-tah) of his initia-tion as an angakoq when he learned the songs of the two great hill spirits. He had become famous serving as a guide for Piulissuaq (Robert Peary) in his incompre-hensible search for the Navel of the Earth, the Big Nail or North Pole. In 1910, he had been one of the murderers of Uisaakassak, the Big Liar who had attempted to describe the marvels of New York with such disastrous results.

A few days later, Malaurie found Odark still attempting to comprehend his new world, attempting to find comparisons to his old way of life.

> An engine, an airplane, is very lovely, very complicated. But we are not impressed. You white men have equipment, books. But we—without knowing much, look what we've been able to do with nothing, not a piece of wood or iron except for what is in Savigssivik [where there is a deposit of meteoric iron]. A sledge, an igloo, is also a very good thing. . . . We have been here for hundreds and hundreds of years. We have some say, some right to speak—after all, this is our home. I'm the oldest of them all. . . . Oh! if Piuli were alive, I would go talk to him. . . . We

Inuit helped the Amerikanski a lot, Piulissuaq, Tatsekuuk, Kane. . . . I'll remind them that we have some rights over them.

Odark realizes that in this extremity it is futile to call on his old helping spirits, the two little men as tall as his thumb that he could summon in lonely places by rubbing a stone on a rock for hours and days on end. Instead he invokes the most powerful name-spirits that he has known, the American explorers Robert Peary, Dr. Frederick Cook and Elisha Kane.

The story of Robert Peary's singleminded obsession to be the first at the North Pole is a revealing chapter in the history of publicity more than in the history of exploration. When he was asked of what use the Eskimos were to the world, he replied that with their help the world would discover the Pole. Some indication of his values can be read into his report of the moment of success in 1909.

After I had planted the American flag in the ice, I told [Matthew] Henson to time the Eskimos for three rousing cheers, which they gave with the greatest enthusiasm. . . . The Eskimos were childishly delighted with our success. While, of course,

161. Don Maganak Gjoa Haven 1990 *Helping Spirit*
"My helping spirits know my thoughts and my will, and they help me when I give commands" (Odark).

they did not realize its importance fully, or its world-wide significance, they did understand that it meant the final achievement of a task upon which they had seen me engaged for many years.

We have a second quite different account of these events from Peter Freuchen, who came to know very well the four Eskimos who accompanied Peary on his final journey. Somehow it is not surprising to learn that they were not childishly delighted with Peary's achievement.

> Odark and the other Eskimos who had been with him could not share his excitement. They had not seen any hole or any other sign of a navel, they complained to their friends. On their way north they had agreed to be particularly careful when they arrived to avoid sliding down the hole and disappearing into the earth, but there was no such danger. They had simply travelled over a vast expanse of ice when Piuli had suddenly announced that he had looked at the sun and found out that they did not have to go any further. Right below them was "The Navel of the Earth" — or the North Pole, as he called it.
>
> For the first time the Eskimos had been disappointed in Peary. Although he was a great man who "thought for them all," they had now seen him take great trouble and travel so far for no reason at all. For years he had dreamed of reaching this very spot, Piuli told them, and the Eskimos wondered at his foolish words for there was nothing to be seen, no animals to hunt, no reason suddenly to return. Since Piuli was a good man who gave them great gifts, they decided to explain to him the childishness of travelling north for days and then, in the middle of the ice — in the middle of nothing — deciding that he was satisfied. They shook their heads in dismay. . . .

Odark had accompanied Peary on several previous expeditions, the first in 1898, but he had never understood the motivations of the outsider. Following Inuit values, he and the others had deferred to Peary's assertiveness and determination, accepting him as an isumatok, "the one who takes thought." To explain to Piuli the childishness of his quest would have been a task almost as arduous as the journey to the pole.

There is a record of an earlier encounter between these two strong-willed men when they met and communicated on close to equal terms. In his previous attempt in 1906 to reach the North Pole, Peary was forced to turn back with Henson and six Inuit at latitude 87°14', several hundred miles from his goal. One decade later, Rasmussen recorded his friend Odaq's (Odark's) account of a dramatic confrontation at the turning point. The small group had been delayed by open water and terrible blizzards in biting cold. Despite these conditions, any lulls in the storms saw a grimly determined Peary making his way ever northward with the worn-out men and dogs trailing behind.

> Then came an evening after such a day when a longing for land, for wife and children and the delicious game far down southward seized the young hunters so strongly that they could see only death and destruction in all their desperate push northwards. They had not spoken much about it; but Odaq thought they looked so strangely at each other; and it struck him that none of them dared to mention land anymore. He could bear it no longer, and went into the snow-hut where

Peary lay sleeping. "I have come to speak to you for my comrades' sake," he said, "for further progress now would mean death for all of us, and I know that you will not turn. Send my comrades back; with the aid of the compass they will be able to find land, and I will go on with you so that you may not die alone."

And Odaq continued: "Then Peary looked at me with such strange sadness, and it seemed to me that for the first time in all the days I had travelled with him his stern eyes looked kind; and he gave me a slap on the shoulder to signify that he understood me, and answered: "I am glad Odaq, for what you have said, but it is not necessary. Tomorrow we will turn. You see, Odaq, neither have I any desire to die now, for another time I shall reach the goal which I must now give up."

After this first meeting of minds, there followed some incredible hardships and near escapes from death as they struggled to return to land and to reach their support ship. Looking back on their experiences, Odark did not dwell on their many difficulties. With characteristic humour, he said, "Oh, well, that was when we were forced to eat our dogs raw, far from land, right out on the ice, while our enormous stores of meat were rotting at home in our camps." Only two years later, Odark and the others were ready to set out again, knowing very well the hazards that they would meet.

Writing about these events after more than ten years had passed, Rasmussen predicted that Peary would become a hero in the myths of the Polar Eskimo. In the decades that have followed, the stories about the great Piuli have been repeated countless times in northern Greenland, but the hero of these tales is more often the skilled hunter and powerful angakoq who made possible the journeys in search of the Navel of the Earth. Two generations later, the explorer and author Wally Herbert learned from Inuutersuaq the story of the desperate struggle to reach land in 1906 as told to him by his lifelong friend Oodaaq (Odark).

One day at last they caught sight of land after they had passed through the freezing fog from the large holes in the ice. . . . Their spirits were high because they knew that they would reach the ship before any of them died of starvation.

There was now hardly anything left of their provisions, but fortunately it was not too far to land. At last the sun broke through and its rays shone down on them. They were looking forward very much to reaching land. They knew of course how many provisions there were at Cape Columbia. Piulerssuaq got busy. Now finally he could read the sun's altitude. His followers were very anxious because they did not know exactly where Cape Columbia lay. When Piulerssuaq had finished looking at the sun the others could see how his spirits had dropped. He turned to them and pointed with an outstretched arm in the direction where there was no land to be seen and said: "The ship is that way." The constant west wind had driven them towards the northern part of Peary Land. Piulerssuaq insisted that they should head for the ship. But for once Oodaaq contradicted him.

. . ."If we set out today for the ship we will certainly die gradually like dogs within three or five days. Die of starvation!" said Oodaaq to the others. "Today we must eat what is left of our food, even if it does not satisfy our hunger! We have to reach land now. If there are animals here, they are our only hope of survival."

The others agreed and Peary brightened up.

Inuutersuaq and the other Inuit told Herbert that they believed Odark's version of the events. They said that he had no reason or need to lie. Reading this account, it is impossible not to recall Kiviung exploring the boundaries of the human world and his long struggle to reach the land. The one hope of survival for both Odark and Kiviung was to reach the shore as soon as possible.

What were Odark's motivations in accepting the challenges and hardships of Peary's expeditions over more than a decade? Attempting to understand Odark's willingness to test the limits of his endurance, Rasmussen pointed to a spirit of adventure and the great gifts that the outsider promised. "They thought it good fun to risk something with a man like Peary — the great Peary of the strong will, the mighty lord of inexhaustible wealth, Piulerssuaq, who himself will surely someday be the hero of one of their tribal myths." Without any doubt, these were contributing factors, but there was very probably a less obvious and much deeper reason. It would be hard not to conclude that in seeking to travel with Piuli to the North Pole, Odark and the others believed that they were engaged in a profound spiritual quest.

To communicate with the Polar Eskimos, Peary depended on his assistant Matthew Henson, who understood their thought processes much better than his employer ever did. Henson earned their respect by learning to hunt, to drive a dog team and to speak fluently the language of the people. As a Black American, he found a freedom and acceptance during his years in northern Greenland that were denied to him at home in the United States. In 1902, it was his task to persuade the Inuit to leave the shore for the first time to venture onto the pack ice with all its dangers. Henson endeavoured to convince them that something called the United States Navy was the "greatest and most powerful devil in the sea." He told them that Peary could invoke its mighty power since he was the "highest honoured son of the Navy." This explained the source of Peary's great wealth and his invincible will. Some of the hunters he employed wore amulets to protect themselves from his powers. The name Piuli that they gave to the outsider was an obvious concession to pronounceability but, more significantly, it reflected the impression made by his boundless wealth. "Piuli, piuli, piuli!" is the cry of the dovekie, the small sea bird that nests in countless numbers in northern Greenland in early June. The return of the dovekies signalled the beginning of a carefree period of abundant food supplies. Peary's expeditions arrived in the northern Arctic at the same time as the dovekie, bringing even greater riches. Years later, the Polar Eskimos heard the dovekie's cry as a reminder of their wealthy visitor.

What did the Polar Eskimos know about the domain far from the shore to which they were being asked to travel? "There is a giant spirit who lives in the north. When he blows his breath, violent snowstorms occur. . . ." This is the beginning of the Labrador Eskimo story recorded by E. W. Hawkes that describes the origin of the winds. Among the Copper Eskimo far to the west, the old angakoq Ilatsiak was famous for the knowledge of the invisible spirit world that he had acquired after a lifetime's experiences. However, as he admitted to Diamond Jenness with some concern, he did not know what became of the winds in calm weather. Where was the home of Sila and the other dangerous spirits when the people lived in peaceful harmony with these unseen forces?

162. Manasie Akpaliapik   Arctic Bay c. 1988   *Sila*
The Great Spirit of the Air is represented with flowing hair that gives rise to winds and
storms. Manasie chose the beige-coloured stone for the base as a reminder of the steep
cliffs of Arctic Bay where the wind howls and whistles loudly during a storm.

During the Sedna festival among the Central Eskimo of Baffin Island, the celebrants made two solemn wishes; "They wish for calm weather and that the souls in their bodies may be calm, like the weather, for then they will be healthy and have long life." These wishes, Ilatsiak's concern, and the Labrador Eskimo story all expressed the desire to live in harmony with an incomprehensible nature. In a song recorded by Raymond de Coccola, the hunter Kakagun deals with the same desire.

> Aya, aya, ayhe . . .
> Hilla, Hilla, where are you?
> Hiding behind the hills and in the clouds?
> Hilla, Hilla, where do you run to?
> To the end of the seas, or to the heavens?
> Aya, aya, aya, ayhe . . .
> I know where you are,
> I know where you go,
> I know where you run,
> And I won't give you peace!
> Aya, aya, aya, ayhe, e, e, e . . .

Kakagun's confident boasts are not completely convincing, but a shaman must show no fear in his confrontation with the spirit world. The Aivilik angakoq Aua posed the great question with urgent directness: "In order to hunt well and live happily, man must have calm weather. Why this constant succession of blizzards and all this needless hardship for men seeking food for themselves and those they care for? Why? Why?"

Donald MacMillan was one of the many volunteers who assisted Peary on the final attempt to reach the North Pole. He asked himself why the Inuit would want to go on the expedition and concluded that it was certainly not for money or goods. They were promised all supplies needed for their work and a reward of a new Winchester rifle, but if their dogs were killed they were not to be replaced. If the Inuit returned to their homes, it would be late in the summer with little time left to hunt to fill the meat caches for the winter. Carefully analysing this puzzle, MacMillan believed that the Inuit did get something in return for accepting all the terrible hardships. "They joined a circus! They satisfied for a time their desire to roam afield, ever persistent in an Eskimo, by nature a nomad. They experienced adventure, excitement, social life, the very things they crave." What MacMillan seems to be describing here are more the motivations of a young university graduate, a gifted student athlete, facing the prospect of a career as a schoolteacher in Maine.

Writing more than twenty-five years after the events, MacMillan recalled trying to understand the beliefs and fears of the Inuit during the expedition, handicapped by his limited knowledge of Inuktitut.

> They tried to tell me much more that I could not understand, of their customs and ways and the life beyond as we sat in the igloo at the edge of the Polar Sea and listened nightly for Tornarsuit, the evil spirits of the North. Torngak, the greatest of them all, was heard repeatedly. He was in the moaning of the winds, in the rush of

drift, in the cracking of the sea ice. He stood at our door for hours, and even in the snow passage, listening, always listening. We could hear him as he crept softly up over the dome of our snow house so that he might peer through the small four-inch hole at the top. Twice Egingwa, with loaded rifle, dropped through the hole in the floor, stole quietly to the end of the snow passage and fired into the darkness. Yes, he was there! He is always in such places when one is far from home, and it is dark, and the wind blows, and it is cold.

Despite the author's limitations, this is the best description of the real adventure that the Inuit had embarked upon. They were travelling with Peary into the dangerous domain of the Tornarsuit and great Torngak. One night, they seemed to change their minds when an alcohol stove malfunctioned and almost poisoned two of the Inuit. According to MacMillan, "It needed but an experience of this kind to become known generally for the Eskimos, highly wrought up as they were already by the fear of the Evil Spirits of the Polar Sea, to forget loyalty and leave in a body." Peary quelled the rebellion quickly by ordering two of the most fearful to return to land. MacMillan thought he had not been severe enough. "Poo-ad-loo-na, brother of the now famous Oo-tah and smiling Egingwa, deserved to be sent home. He was a quitter and a trouble-maker, as was, in fact, Oo-tah himself, Peary's 'iron man', who professed to be an Angekok." These hasty judgements represent another lost opportunity for understanding.

Among themselves, the Polar Eskimos with Peary were worried about what they would find at the North Pole, the Navel of the Earth. Their fear of, as Freuchen records it, "sliding down the hole and disappearing into the earth" was derived from a common visualization of the helping spirits of an angakoq entering his body through the navel at the moment of inspiration. There was a compelling reason for Odark and his companions to risk the hazards of leaving the shore, a reason far more significant than adventure or the prospect of rewards. They believed that they were seeking the answer to Ilatsiak's concern and Aua's profound question. They were attempting to find the place far from land where the Great Spirit of the Air entered into the body of the earth, the place where Torngak or Sila penetrated all of nature when the weather was calm. We can imagine their dismay when Piuli looked at the sun and announced that they had arrived. There was nothing to be seen, no hole or any sign of a navel. In Odark's mind at that moment, it was Robert Peary who did not understand the worldwide significance of their journey. Both Odark and Peary had risked everything, defying their own natures in their repeated attempts to complete imaginative visions of the world, comprehensive visions of all that exists. Inevitably they had failed, and the measure of their failures was their inability to comprehend each other.

After planting the American flag in the ice, Peary, Henson and the four Polar Eskimos returned with all possible speed to their support ship. Peary gave the following account of the moment when the small party came within sight of land.

> Before midnight that night the whole party had reached the glacial fringe of Grant Land. We had now left the ice of the polar sea and were practically on terra firma. When the last sledge came to the almost vertical edge of the glacier's fringe, I

163. George Arluk   Arviat 1990   *Shining Shaman*
"The spirits of the air saw the shamans in the form of shining bodies that attracted and
drew them and made them wish to go and live in them and give them their own strength,
sight and knowledge. When such a spirit beset a shaman it went in by the navel and
found a place in the breast cavity, whence it inspired him. Compared with the shining
shamans, ordinary people are like houses with extinguished lamps; they are dark inside
and do not attract the attention of the spirits" (Rasmussen 1932, 28).

thought my Eskimos had gone crazy. They yelled and danced until they fell from utter exhaustion. As Ootah sank down on his sledge, he remarked in Eskimo: "The devil is asleep or having trouble with his wife or we should never have come back so easily."

The Eskimos had not gone crazy; they had escaped from the domain of the spirits and returned to the shore. Peary's understanding of the Inuit language and his appreciation of their belief system were never impressive. He once wrote that the Eskimos, strictly speaking, have no religion in our sense of the word. In all probability, Odark meant to say that Sila and Sedna, the Great Spirits of the Air and Sea, were at peace and had allowed the six explorers to return to the human world. We can believe that the Great Spirits had admired the persistence and blind courage of the little men, so alone and vulnerable at the top of the world.

Some months after the events in 1951 described by Malaurie, Peter Freuchen returned to visit Thule and went to talk to his old friend Odark for the last time. When they first met in 1910, Odark feared that Freuchen (a six foot, seven inch giant) had come to punish him for the murder of Uisaakassak, which had occurred only a few days before. He had heard rumours of the new custom that the white men were introducing in Greenland — one was no longer supposed to kill one's enemies. Now they were both old men and Odark poured out his complaints.

Things are not like they used to be, Pita. When we were young and strong, we chased the bear, the seal and the walrus ourselves. We got meat where we wanted it. Today, today the meat is sold for money! I have money enough. The king gives me more than I need, but I shall never stoop to buying my meat. I shall never pay my friends to feed my dogs.

Do you remember when you first came to Thule, Pita? I fed your dogs and I fed them well. Today meat is put on the scales and every morsel is weighed. No longer does a man know how to chase a bear or catch a fish. He waits for the fish to come by itself and swallow a lazy hook. I have never caught any fish but the salmon I stabbed with my spear.

Things are not like they used to be when you were young. Do you remember the house you built in Thule, Pita? The first house you ever built here. Today there is a city of white men, and the noise they make has chased away all living things. No longer does the ice bear cross to Melville Bay, seals and walrus have left for happier hunting grounds, and the wild geese are gone. Life seems a heavier burden than death to me today, Pita. And death cannot be far away when our land is like it is today and when my friends take money for meat!

Although he was well into his seventies, old Odark concluded that they had no choice but to go farther and farther away. The creatures of land, sea and air had already left for happier hunting grounds. Taking money for meat was the final indignity. This new custom did not recognize the moral obligation to share. It broke the sacred relationship between human and animal.

Odark knew what had to be done, but first he had to resolve one last inner conflict. He admitted to Freuchen that life had become easier with the coming of the white men. It was no longer necessary for them to kill their children in times of starvation, and old people did not become burdens to the young. Very recently, the king had given him a small house and a doubled pension as belated rewards for his many contributions to arctic exploration. It had taken the Danish government more than forty years to decide finally to overlook the murder of Uisaakassak.

> I need my peace, Pita. I need to sit quietly in my house and contemplate the old days when I went with the great Piuli to the Navel of the Earth. Our trip took many, many weeks and it called for the strength and courage of men. Today they fly in a machine to the Navel of the Earth and it takes no courage! . . .
>
> We go farther north. New men have moved in. They know not the old ways. They have little peace or dignity. They have taken the land. But our land is great — we move on. . . . One day you will see there is less happiness in the land of the white man. . . . We are being punished because we have stayed too long in one place, Pita. Life is journey without end!

There is a Polar Eskimo saying that it is not possible to attach a man to the land until death overtakes him and ties his body to a stone mound. According to another saying, a man is always ready for a long journey. The old angakoq has never forgotten these proverbs and he realizes that he needs more than a comfortable life. "Today they fly in a machine to the Navel of the Earth and it takes no courage!" Where is the dignity or joy in such a life? Whatever the cost, Odark chooses the life of a man, a life that tests the inner resources of strength and courage. He chooses to confront the old dangers and the old spirits until the end.

9. Afterword

THE IMAGINATIVE world of the Inuit is too large a subject to be captured in a few pages or to be illustrated by a few sculptures. In this short space, we have attempted to develop or at least to outline two themes. First, the visual art created by so many hands in the last four decades has been a genuine expression of the unique Inuit imagination. And second, there is a precedent for this out-pouring of creativity in the role of songs and storytelling in traditional life.

Many observers have emphasized the crucial role of the simplest narratives and songs in daily life. The importance of this activity was eloquently expressed by the Netsilik shaman Orpingalik who described his songs as his "comrades in loneliness." When Rasmussen asked how many songs he had created, he replied, "I cannot tell you, for I do not know how many there are of these songs of mine. Only I know that there are many, and that all in me is song. I sing as I draw breath." One of these Netsilik songs uses a familiar image to describe the diffi-culties of composition in a very self-conscious way.

> I wonder why
> My song-to-be that I wish to use,
> My song-to-be that I wish to put together,
> I wonder why it will not come to me.
> At Sioraq it was at a fishing hole in the ice,
> I could feel a little trout on the line,
> And then it was gone.
> I stood jigging.
> But why is it so difficult, I wonder?
> When summer came and the waters opened,
> It was then that catching became so hard.
> I am not good at hunting.

At first, Orpingalik had been reluctant to share his magic songs and spells, but he relented when Rasmussen offered to trade some of the songs that he had acquired from Aua. They agreed that the magic power would not be harmed since it was a white man who served as the medium of conveyance.

Fifteen years after Rasmussen, Gontran de Poncins spent a few weeks with the Netsilik Inuit living near Pelly Bay. His guide Nibtayok took him on a tour of the widely scattered hunting camps. Their first visit was a memorable encounter with Nibtayok's father. "[He] was a very interesting old man, one of the few, even up here, who clung to the old ways. For example, he still hunted the cari-bou with bow and arrow. His name had once been Orpingalik; now he called himself Alakannoak. . . . [He] came across to me and raised my hand with the greatest grace. Then he went over to his son. But to my astonishment, Nibtayok turned away and pretended to be watching something on the horizon. Later, I

164. Charlie Ugyuk Spence Bay 1975 *Devil*
This is a story about the demons that come with drinking. Charlie Ugyuk said that when
he starts drinking he seems to enjoy himself. He made the carving very small to show
that you do not see the evil coming.

asked if they had quarrelled, this father and son. Not at all. It was a long time since they had seen each other, and the son had been too shy to look his father in the face." For his own reasons, Orpingalik as an old man had returned to hunting caribou with bow and arrow. When he encountered Rasmussen earlier, he was on his way to Repulse Bay to trade fox skins for a rifle to replace one that he had lost.

Among the Netsilik Inuit, Rasmussen claimed that he rarely saw men or women at work without their humming a song. Even children engaged in this necessary outlet for creative impulses. "They all have their songs, both men and women. And sometimes it happens that children, half in play, half in earnest, make up songs and deliver them among playmates when playing song festivals in a little snowhut they have built themselves." Not every outside observer was prepared to appreciate these songs and their role in Inuit life. The Norwegian explorer Roald Amundsen was icebound in his ship *Gjoa* for almost two years from 1903 to 1905 in the land of the Netsilik. He made the same observations as Rasmussen, but his reaction was quite different. "Eskimo always sing while at work, if I may describe the sounds they emit as 'singing.' . . . Even to one whose highest musical achievement consists in singing a nursery rhyme out of tune, this monotonous music was maddening. However, when I visited them they always stopped singing, as they knew their unmusical performance at once incited me to imitation, and rather than hear me, they lapsed into silence." There is a good possibility that Orpingalik was one of the singers whose monotonous music disturbed Amundsen.

So widespread and natural was the urge to create songs that some Inuit could not imagine a culture in which songs had a different significance.

> I shall never forget Ivaluardjuk's astonishment and confusion when I tried to explain to him that in our country there were people who devoted themselves exclusively to the production of poems and melodies. His first attempt at an explanation of this inconceivable suggestion was that such persons must be great shamans who had perhaps attained to some intimate relationship with the spirits. But as soon as he was informed that our poets were not shamans, merely people who handled words, thoughts and feelings according to the technique of a particular art, the problem appeared altogether beyond him.

There is much more to be said about the sources of songs and poems in these very different cultures. As usual, Shakespeare, in a famous passage from *A Midsummer Night's Dream*, has said it best for the outsiders.

> The poet's eye, in a fine frenzy rolling,
> Doth glance from heaven to earth, from earth to heaven,
> And as imagination bodies forth
> The form of things unknown, the poet's pen
> Turns them into shapes, and gives to airy nothing
> A local habitation, and a name.
> Such tricks hath strong imagination,
> That if it would but apprehend some joy,
> It comprehends some bringer of that joy.

> Or in the night, imagining some fear,
> How easy is a bush supposed a bear!

"The lunatic, the lover, and the poet are of imagination all compact." Hearing these lines instead of Rasmussen's pedestrian account, Ivaluardjuk might have concluded that our poets were shamans after all. The angakoq Orpingalik also used some images as evocative as Shakespeare's to express his ideas on the sources of his compositions.

> Songs are thoughts which are sung out with the breath when the people let themselves be moved by a great force, and ordinary speech no longer suffices.
>
> A person is moved like an ice-floe which drifts with the current. His thoughts are driven by a flowing force when he feels joy, when he feels fear, when he feels sorrow. Thoughts can surge in on him, causing him to gasp for breath, and making his heart beat faster. Something like a softening of the weather will keep him thawed. And then it will happen that we, who always think of ourselves as small, will feel even smaller. And we will hesitate before using words. But it will happen that the words we need will come of themselves.

By now, we understand what the singer means to convey by "a softening of the weather." It is the peace that is granted when we live in harmony with our own natures and the unseen forces. Orpingalik concluded by saying, "When the words that we need shoot up of themselves, we have a new song."

It was old Ivaluardjuk, the brother of Aua, who expressed his feelings for the life he had known with unforgettable nostalgia. "When I was young, every day was a beginning of some new thing and every evening ended with the glow of the next day's dawn. Now I have only the old stories and songs to fall back on, the songs I sang myself in the days when I delighted to challenge my comrades to a song contest in the feasting house." This nostalgia for the past life that is so evident in modern Inuit art is also expressed very poignantly in an old song.

> There is fear
> In the longing for loneliness
> When gathered with friends
> And longing to be alone.
> Iyaiya-yaya!
>
> There is joy
> In feeling the summer
> Come to the great world
> And watching the sun
> Follow its ancient way.
> Iyaiya-yaya!
>
> There is fear
> In feeling the winter
> Come to the great world
> And watching the moon
> Now half-moon, now full,
> Follow its ancient way.
> Iyaiya-yaya!

165. Anonymous   Gjoa Haven 1980   *Magic Song*
"From men of the first times, various incantations have been handed down to appease or drive away the malignant spirits.... Many of the incantations are very old and have lost whatever meaning they had originally, but this does not lessen their potency" (Jenness, 187). The barely visible bird spirit on the reverse of the sculpture carries the singer's magic breath to the spirit world.

Whither is all this tending?
I would I were far to the eastward.
And yet I shall never again
Meet with my kinsman.
Iyaiya-yaya!

From simple sayings to ancient myths, Inuit folklore is oriented toward social solidarity, expressing imaginatively this longing to "meet with my kinsman" or Nibtayok's desire to "look his father in the face." In all cultures, the framework of stories defines the limits of appropriate behaviour or what it means to be human.

Storytelling is an art of communication at both conscious and subconscious levels, but it is not unique among the arts in this characteristic. The renowned critic Bernard Berenson viewed all art as communication but subject to some essential requirements. "Communication is made possible by accepted conventions and by these only, and the history of all expression, of all the arts, and of the visual arts in particular, should be, can be, nothing but an account and perhaps an attempt to interpret its successive conventions. A tradition, a convention needs constant manipulation to vivify it, to enlarge it, to keep it fresh and supple, and capable of generating problems and producing their solution." In Berenson's terms, Ivaluardjuk was unable to comprehend the conventions by which poems and melodies were produced in a culture alien to his experience. Many critics of contemporary Inuit art have similarly failed to understand the cultural conventions and traditions that have given rise to it. The artists, on the other hand, have seized the opportunities presented by the new forms. Using the profound symbols and images made available by the traditional culture, they have been able to express themes with great personal meaning.

In the early years of this century, the Anglican missionary Julian Bilby suspected that Inuit culture would find its artistic expression in literature. "It is for the future to reveal whether or not the newly found gift of writing will lead these people on to extensive literature. . . . If so, by the analogy of every literature in the world, it will begin with verse, by the enshrining of the folk tales immemorially dear to every nation, and by the composition of some sort of Eskimo saga." To date, this has not happened, at least not in a literary form. Very little literature has been produced in the Canadian north. Instead, visual art has continued the oral tradition to modern times but in a different form. This is less surprising when we remember that, in its original context, Inuit storytelling was a highly visual performance art. However, looking ahead, George Swinton has speculated that "in a world of words, the future of Eskimo art may well become more verbal than visual." To a great extent, this has already occurred in Greenland where the authors' union has more than one hundred active members and there is a rapidly growing literature.

Any account of the Inuit imagination of former times must begin and end with the sensitive observations of Knud Rasmussen. His works can be called an epic of the traditional life, the Eskimo saga expected by Bilby. Before deciding to dedicate his life to ethnography, he tried his hand briefly at three other careers — acting, singing and journalism — the European training of an angakoq. Uniquely

166. Charlie Ugyuk   Spence Bay c. 1990   *Bad Spirits*
Christianity was forced on us, according to the artist, and the angakoqs came to be seen
as devils. He thinks that the Inuit were criticized and condemned for beliefs that were
really not part of the traditional culture and religion.

among all descriptions of Inuit culture, Rasmussen's writings recognize the full amplitude of the spiritual dimension, the latent resource that has found its creative expression in visual art in recent times.

> True, they say themselves that a man's only business is to procure food and clothing, and while fulfilling his duties in this respect he finds, in his hunting and adventures, the most wonderful experiences of his life. Nevertheless, men may be to the highest degree interested in spiritual things; and I am thinking here not only of their songs and poems, their festivals when strangers come to their place, but also of the manner in which they regard religious questions, wherein they evince great adaptability and versatility. This it is which always gives their accounts that delightful originality which is the peculiar property of those whose theories are based on experience of life itself. Their naturalness makes of them philosophers and poets unawares, and their simple and primitive orthodoxy gives to their presentment of a subject a childlike charm which makes even the mystic element seem credible.

When he writes that Inuit thought is based on experience of life itself, Rasmussen is summarizing his own observations, but he is also quoting the angakoq Aua who told him, "Our customs come from life and are directed towards life; we cannot explain; we do not believe in this or that." Their customs did come from their intense experience, but their understanding of life included the supernatural. The Netsilik woman Nalungiark told Rasmussen that she had never seen visions. After recounting her version of the story of Nuliajuk, she concluded by saying humbly, "That is all I can tell you about the world, both the one I know and the one I do not know. If only I could dream I would know more; for people who can dream, hear and see many things. We believe in dreams, and we believe that people can live a life apart from real life, a life they can go through in their sleep."

As a young man, Peter Freuchen caught a glimpse of the hidden forces in the Inuit way of life at an ecstatic song festival. He then set himself the task of learning as much as he could of the secrets which lay dormant in their souls. Many years later, he admitted defeat. "Though I spent more than half a century with the Eskimos, I do not believe that I ever completely understood them. Their souls had depths almost impossible for a white man to penetrate. . . . When you penetrate a little below the smiling amiability of the Eskimo, a deep violent fantasy is revealed, a profoundly reasoned speculation on the conditions and circumstances of his life." Freuchen was constantly impressed by the simplicity and dignity of Inuit customs. He recorded one memorable demonstration of these qualities.

> On the rock of Agpat, behind Thule, where the dead ones are stone-set, I often saw men and women sit in quiet meditation. On these occasions, they would dress in their newest and most beautiful clothes, and then sit still, staring out over land and sea for hours on end. They believed that during this stillness they received the wisdom of the ancestors. It is the only thing approximating religious devotion I have seen among them, but also — I think — the most beautiful form of devotion I have ever seen.

In his writings, Freuchen had the Inuit ability to compress emotion and meaning

167. David Ruben Piqtoukun   Paulatuk, Toronto 1992   *Dog Child*
Shown as part human, the dog child is on the way to becoming a white man or Indian.
Piqtoukun attempted to show the nervousness and fear the dog child and contemporary
Inuit feel at the prospect of a journey away from the world they know.

168. Manasie Akpaliapik   Arctic Bay 1989   *Man Losing Soul*
A work that does not represent the shaman's flight, this sculpture makes a contemporary
comment. The nail in the mouth symbolizes the self-inflicted damage of drugs and their
power to take your soul away. In the old days, the angakoqs could enter the ecstatic state
now achieved by using drugs. The new way can lead to losing the sense of reality
permanently.

169. David Ruben Piqtoukun   Paulatuk, Toronto 1992   *Seven Stones*
The shaman's soul is leaving his body lying within a tent ring, seven stones representing
the bondage to the human world. The stones have been used to hold down a tent. They
may be used again to surround a final resting place.

into a single resonant image. Near the end of his life, he recalled the countless times he had made his way across the ice of Melville Bay using Black Mountain behind Thule as a navigational beacon.

> How many times I had looked at the landmark, how many times I had hated the dark hostile mountain which was always so far away. When the snow was deep and the dogs were tired, when the ice seemed impassable under a cold hard moon and lack of food sapped all one's strength, Black Mountain was always there, always as far away as ever. Time and again I had forced myself not to look up, not to watch the distant landmark before I felt it must have moved closer. When hours had gone by, after a whole day's painful march, the distant goal was as far away as ever. But I had learned to ignore it, to keep going after the distant goal, never to give up.

When Freuchen died in Alaska in 1957, his remains were cremated and the ashes returned to Greenland to be scattered over the mountains behind his beloved Thule. We are free to believe that he is now one of the "great hill-spirits, as tall as a tent" described by the young Odark, always ready to disturb the dreams of the unwary.

Many others have been greatly affected by the deep meaning of the sincere rituals of Inuit life. Raymond de Coccola described the last rites for old Igutak, the husband of Oviluk, in words that need no additional comment. After his sudden death in a hunting accident, his body had rested for two days near his tent so that his soul would not feel neglected and turn angrily against his family. On the third day, Igutak's body was loaded onto his sled and taken to the same lookout point from which a few days before they had joyfully observed the arrival of the great herds of caribou.

> Krilugok helped Nerlak unload his sled, placing Igutak's body on an elevation with a perfect view of the valley below. It lay there facing the sun, the source of life. Oviluk knelt close to the opening of the bundle where Igutak's face could be seen. She leaned forward and breathed around his face, simultaneously touching his nostrils and mouth as she murmured and called his soul to come forth, "Come, oh come! And go up into the mountains until your name is given to a newborn. . . . Go down into the valley and follow the roaming caribou until your name rests with the newborn."
>
> Symbolically she placed the beak of a falcon on her deceased husband's mouth to give his soul the bird's power to fly at will to the hills or the lowlands.
>
> Around Igutak's frozen body the two men placed a ring of stone to guard it against roaming spirits, always on the prowl in the Barren Land. As he helped complete the stone circle, Krilugok said the magic words, "Troublesome Spirits of the Air and Land, turn away and return to the dark."

Some of Igutak's most valued possessions were then placed inside the ring of stones—an old hunting rifle, a tin of tobacco, a bow, some arrows and a copper hook with its fishing line—to help him on his final journey. Father de Coccola observed this scene in silence, realizing that there was nothing in his religion that could add to the dignity of the ritual that he had been privileged to witness.

The meditation on life and death implicit in Inuit beliefs and customs has an

170. David Ruben Piqtoukun
Paulatuk, Toronto 1992
Death of the Old Spirits
The intention of this work was to bring to
mind the contest between the old beliefs and
Christianity as indicated by the cross form.
The angakoq's inua is leaving his body in the
form of a bear spirit, perhaps for the last time.

171. Pauta Saila   Cape Dorset 1992
Dancing Bear
Always called Pauta bears, these carefully
balanced creatures suggest the angakoq
poised between heaven and earth, ready for
transformation and flight. Pauta explained
that a shamanic bear can be recognized by a
short thick neck, the one remaining sign of
human identity.

appeal that affects us at a level not subject to rigorous analysis and explanation. Franz Boas was initially trained as a geographer and cartographer, but, like Freuchen, after his early arctic experience he dedicated his long career to mapping the mental universes of primitive peoples. In his study *Primitive Art*, he reminds us that the logic of primitive thought is in fact universal. "Investigators are too apt to forget that the logics of science — that unattainable ideal of the discovery of pure relations of cause and effect, uncontaminated by any kind of emotional bias as well as of unproved opinion — are not the logics of life. The feelings underlying taboo are ever present among us. . . . Our advantage over primitive people is one of greater knowledge of the objective world, painfully gained by the labour of many generations, a knowledge which we apply rather badly and which we, or at least most of us, discard just as soon as a strong emotional urge impels us to do so, and for which we substitute forms quite analogous to those of primitive thought." Despite what science teaches, the sun rises in the east and the heart rules the head. The hissing sounds of the northern lights can be heard by those who know how to listen. When spoken in the right way, there is a magic power in the songs and stories of traditional Inuit life. They lead away from the desire to explain and control everything. They help us to regain the spiritual dimension and a feeling of humility in our relations to the world. They help us to recognize opportunities to transform ourselves, to revive our understanding of the core of our human identity.

After their long journey ended in Alaska, Rasmussen and his two Inuit companions returned to civilization quickly, travelling by steamship from Nome to Seattle and by train across the continent. A month later he stood with Miteq and Anarulunguaq on the roof of a skyscraper in New York looking out over a "stony desert," the same unreal landscape that Uisaakassak had attempted to describe twenty-five years before.

> "Ah," sighed Anarulunguaq, "and we used to think Nature was the greatest and most wonderful of all! Yet here we are among mountains and great gulfs and precipices, all made by the work of human hands. Nature is great; Sila, as we used to call it at home; nature, the world, the universe, all that is Sila; which our wise men declared they could hold in poise. And I could never believe it; but I see it now. Nature is great; but are not men greater? Those tiny beings we can see down there far below, hurrying this way and that. They live among these stone walls; on a great plain of stones made with hands. Stone and stone and stone — there is no game to be seen anywhere, and yet they manage to live and find their daily food. Have they then learned of the animals, since they can dig down under the earth like marmots, hang in the air like spiders, fly like the birds and dive under water like fishes; seemingly masters of all that we struggled against ourselves?
>
> I see things more than my mind can grasp; and the only way to save oneself from madness is to suppose that we have all died suddenly before we knew, and this is part of another life."

The profound words of Anarulunguaq — "Nature is great; but are not men greater?" — were repeated by Rasmussen to end *Across Arctic America*, his popular account of the Fifth Thule Expedition. With penetrating insight, Anarulunguaq suggests that, by learning from the animals, the white men have broken through the barriers separating the human and animal worlds. Inuit narratives are the imaginative record of the ceaseless struggle to avoid this fate.

With feelings of satisfaction and regret, Rasmussen saw that the greatest journey of his life was at an end. Facing the prospect of several years of monotonous toil organizing thousands of artifacts and rewriting the contents of thirty large notebooks, he allowed himself one heartfelt sigh; "Alas, what are words compared with life itself!" The great explorer also saw very clearly that the journey of the two Greenlanders and all Inuit into the unknown territory of another life was just beginning. He did not believe that Miteq and Anarulunguaq would be able to return to their old ways after their new experiences. He may have underestimated the hold of the traditional life and its resilience.

Returning in 1907 from an expedition on Ellesmere Island to hunt muskoxen, Rasmussen and two Polar Eskimo companions came across the tracks of two sledges. They knew immediately that the tracks had been made by the families returning to their homes after assisting Peary in his unsuccessful assault on the North Pole one year before. They recognized the tracks of two men, two women and two small children; "'Look, the little ones have walked that long, long way,' said one of the Eskimos when he saw the children's tracks. 'Our women bear strong children!' cried the other one, examining the tracks as he ran." When they caught up to the sledges, they found two families: Aqpalinguaq with his wife, a small daughter, and an almost new born baby; Odark and his wife, a little son of five years, and a baby-in-arms.

Considering what these families had experienced in the past year, they seemed to be remarkably healthy and contented as they walked toward their goal.

> These Arctic travellers all looked like people who are returning from a little pleasure trip, well fed and smilingly healthy. The women and the little ones had just finished a walking tour of a hundred miles, the mothers with their smallest on their backs, and all of them had for more than a month been a prey to the cold and the sweeping blizzards out on the ice. And if a blast is to be found anywhere in Greenland you will find it by Humboldt's Glacier — a blast with a bite in it. Another eight families were still on the way; two sledges had dropped a little behind the others, delayed because the women that accompanied them gave birth to their children whilst travelling. They told us in this manner, quietly and as a matter of fact, without any attempt to be sensational.

Rasmussen admitted that in his years in the north he had never felt smaller than when faced by these child-bearing women, cheerfully accepting the hardships of a journey that would have cost many a white man his life. In their quest to find the Navel of the Earth, Odark and the others had failed but, like Kiviung, they had returned to the shore. They would not fail in the struggle to return to their homes.

Let us end our exploration with an image created by Luke Iksiktaaryuk, an artist whose life span from 1909 to 1977 encompassed the great changes in Inuit life. He was one of the proud group of Harvaqtormiut (People of the Eddies) that moved to Baker Lake in the late 1950s at a time of starvation. This group of Caribou Eskimo was the first that Rasmussen encountered when he set out

172. Luke Iksiktaaryuk   Baker Lake c. 1972   *Difficult Journey*
A simplified composition that expresses the hardships of the Inuit existence and the
courageous determination to overcome them by accepting the difficulties of the endless
journey.

173. Luke Iksiktaaryuk   Baker Lake c. 1976   *Name Spirit*
An old man has lost his breath. His name spirit lingers about the land he has known and
the small group of people that has shared his joys and sorrows. His name cannot be
spoken until it lives again in a newborn child.

inland from Baker Lake in 1922. As they approached the small settlement, all the women and children disappeared into the igloos. Only two men remained outside. The visitor knew the proper greeting for the occasion, "I come from the right side," meaning that they came as friends. As soon as these words were spoken, "the two men sprang up with loud cries and came running toward us, while the remainder of the party came tumbling from their huts." Many of them had never seen a white man before. Rasmussen learned that the preceding winter had been very severe with several deaths from starvation.While he was there, word reached the settlement that the first caribou had been sighted. All their hardships were immediately forgotten. "In a moment the entire assembly was in a turmoil of extravagant rejoicing. Here was the end of winter; the caribou were come, and with them summer and its abundance."

Iksiktaaryuk's carving style was unique; simple but expressive human figures, individually or in groups, carved from caribou antler, a material that is in itself a symbol of birth and regeneration. The work illustrated is one of the last that he made before his death. It is an ambiguous image that may represent the courageous flight of the shaman to the spirit world to find the causes of the difficulties afflicting the community. We prefer to believe that it represents the spirit of an old man who has lost his breath but is not forgotten. His name-spirit lingers about the community and land that he has known, waiting impatiently until it enters a new life. Then, when the newborn child takes its first breath and calls out for its name, the joyful cry "*inuulirivuq!*" will be heard once more. Great Sila will carry the word that carries all meaning, "he lives again!"

REFERENCES

1. Inuit Stories

15 Boas 1964, 164
    Rasmussen 1927, 11
    Fleming, 379
16 de Coccola, 30
    Rasmussen 1927, 25
17 Freuchen 1935, 392
    Rasmussen 1927, 252, 90; 1930a, 87
18 de Coccola, 26
    Boas 1964, 233
19 Jenness 223, 32
20 de Poncins 257, 31
    Freuchen 1953, 188
    van den Steenhoven, 99
    Pryde, 142, 84
22 Schwarz, 68
    Nungak and Arima, 3, 39
    Turner, 99
    Rasmussen 1927, 170, 238
    de Coccola, 231
23 Turner, 97-100
28 Turner, 22
29 Schwarz, 76
    Rasmussen 1930a, 83
    Turner, 96
    de Coccola, 80
30 Carpenter in Vallee, 41
    Jenness, 230
    de Poncins, 167, 252
32 Swinton 1972, 140
    Fleming, 100
    Marsh, 163
    de Coccola, 373

2. The Spirit World

33 Rasmussen 1932, 124; 1927, 254; 1908, 99
    Birket-Smith, 57
    Jenness, 217
    Rasmussen 1930b, 69
34 Freuchen 1961, 230
36 Freuchen 1961, 80, 208
    Jenness, 168, 189
    Rasmussen 1927, 81, 70
    de Coccola, 80
37 Turner, 102
    Iglauer, 64

38 de Coccola, 179, 289
    Jenness, 154, 182
39 Spencer, 266
    Boas 1964, 185; 1975, 161
    Jenness, 185
    Bruemmer, 38
    Pryde, 105
    Rasmussen 1932, 45
    de Coccola, 81
41 Turner, 37
    Rasmussen 1927, 185, 178; 1932, 47
    Jenness, 187
42 de Coccola, 360
43 Hawkes, 162
    Rasmussen 1927, 137
    Birket-Smith, 176
    Rasmussen 1930b, 234
44 Rasmussen 1932, 183; 1927, 24; 1921, 40
46 Turner, 32
    Jenness, 198
    Freuchen 1961, 210
47 Birket-Smith, 181
48 Rasmussen 1908, 17; 1927, 126; 1930b, 77
    Jenness, 92, 191, 193
50 Rasmussen 1908, 147
    Spencer, 318
51 Rasmussen 1927, 81
    Jenness, 205
    Lowenstein, 131
    Rasmussen 1927, 84
52 Marsh, 135
    Rasmussen 1927, 96; 1932, 27; 1930b, 79, 111
56 Jenness, 194
    Rasmussen 1927, 34
57 Boas 1964, 184
61 Boas 1964, 260
62 Boas 1964, 186
    Jenness, 216
    Rasmussen 1927, 96, 122, 128
65 Birket-Smith, 188

3. Sedna and the Shaman's Journey

71 Rasmussen 1927, 195
    N. Swinton, 13
    Rasmussen 1927, 277, 162
72 de Coccola, 16, 244, 10, 8

73 Rasmussen 1927, 27; 1929, 63

76 Freuchen 1935, 434
    de Coccola, 373
    Boas 1964, 175

79 Freuchen 1935, 152

80 Freuchen and Salomensen 1958, 139, 125
    Boas 1964, 178

82 Rasmussen 1929, 208; 1927, 32

83 Boas 1975, 139

84 Rasmussen 1927, 136; 1932, 25

85 Boas 1964, 196

86 Boas 1975, 140

4. Raven, Can You Tell Us The Story?

88 Fleming, 137
    Scherman, 228

90 Wilkinson, 202, 220

92 Wilkinson, 136

95 Freuchen 1961, 152
    Birket-Smith, 57
    Scherman, 126
    Georgia, 172
    Pryde, 188

99 Rasmussen 1932, 51

105 Gilberg 1969
     Freuchen 1935, 51
     Rink, 291

106 Oswalt, 65
     Thomson, 149, 151
     Rasmussen 1921, 15; 1908, 39
     Freuchen 1961, 119, 224
     van den Steenhoven, 23

107 Boas 1964, 229
     Scherman, 228
     Hawkes, 153
     Jenness, 180

108 Boas 1964, 228

109 Scherman, 159
     Rasmussen 1927, 44

112 Rasmussen 1908, 162

115 *Beaver Magazine*, Winter 1963

116 Rasmussen 1908, 97; 1927, 262
     Spencer, 439

119 Freuchen 1961, 230
     Swinton 1972, 200
     Spencer, 384
     Scherman, 112

120 Lowenstein, 101

5. Qaudjaqdjuq, Lumak and Kiviung

122 Boas 1964, 222

123 Rasmussen 1908, 52
     Freuchen 1961, 59; 1954, 82

124 Malaurie, 128
     Rasmussen 1967, 34

125 Houston 1971, 46
     Myers 1977a

128 Rasmussen 1927, 190, 61

129 Freuchen 1935, 42
     Boas 1964, 213

133 Rasmussen 1930, 79

134 Jenness, 190, 205
     Rasmussen 1929, 145, 170; 1930a, 50
     Turner, 101
     Boas 1964, 185

135 de Poncins, 203
     Freuchen 1953, 129
     de Coccola, 385

139 Rasmussen 1932, 53

142 Blodgett and Bouchard, 43
     Rasmussen 1931, 365, 376

6. My Sleep Is Dreamless

143 Iglauer, 117
     Tagoona, 2

144 Swinton 1972, 131
     Rasmussen 1927, 63, 294

145 Rasmussen 1931, 500; 1927, 66, 198
     Williamson, 168
     Butler, 122

146 Eber 1989, 89; 1977
     Rasmussen 1927, 63, 183

148 Butler, 122
     Blodgett and Bouchard, 42
     Boas 1964, 184
     Rasmussen 1931, 265; 1927, 331
     Boas 1964, 59

150 Hawkes, 159
     Fleming, 86, 128, 185

151 Rasmussen 1927, 127
     de Coccola, 425, 431

153 Pryde, 124
     Buliard, 280, 285
     Freuchen 1935, 319; 1961, 187, 192

154 Rasmussen 1927, 39, 112
     Mathiassen 1928, 234

155 Freuchen 1953, 173; 1961, 180, 190; 1935, 394, 422
     Flaherty 1980, 12, 13, 66, 72, 73

158 Rasmussen 1927, 261
    Lowenstein 1973, 83
    van den Steenhoven, 13
    Jenness, 209
159 Rasmussen 1927, 251, 255; 1932, 125
    Jenness, 232
    Scherman, 74
    Georgia, 43
160 Georgia, 33, 90
    Stefansson, 435

7. I Don't Forget My Old Way

161 Rasmussen 1931, 262
    Jenness, 185
    Boas 1975, 496
    Rasmussen 1927, 66
163 Briggs, 59
164 Butler, 122
    Rasmussen 1927, 188, 192, 197, 198
168 Williamson, 161
169 Freuchen 1935, 390
    Rasmussen 1927, 126, 118
    Eber 1989, 111
170 Boas 1975, 509, 152
171 Rasmussen 1927, 191; 1931, 471
    Arima, 41, 43
    Myers 1977b
173 Turner, 97
176 Jenness, 180
    Rasmussen 1927, 89; 1930b, 118
    Myers 1977a
181 Rasmussen 1927, 157

8. Odark's Journey

182 Malaurie, 384, 392

183 Freuchen 1961, 213
    Peary, 296
184 Freuchen 1954, 134
    Rasmussen 1921, 8
185 Herbert, 188
    Rasmussen 1921, 8
186 Herbert, 142
    Freuchen and Salomensen, 197
188 de Coccola, 352
    MacMillan, 61, 62, 138, 180
189 Peary, 315, 63
191 Freuchen 1953, 1, 92
192 Freuchen 1953, 413
    Rasmussen 1921, 209

9. Afterword

193 Rasmussen 1927, 164; 1931, 517
    de Poncins, 254
195 Lowenstein, 146
    Amundsen, 303
    Rasmussen 1929, 233; 1931, 312
196 Rasmussen 1927, 266; 1932, 135
198 Berenson, 13
    Bilby, 183
    Swinton 1972, 144
200 Lowenstein, 127
    Rasmussen 1929, 208
    Freuchen 1961, 84, 184, 193, 209
204 Freuchen 1953, 414
    de Coccola, 204
207 Boas 1955, 2, 4
    Rasmussen 1927, 387
208 Rasmussen 1921, 11
211 Rasmussen 1927, 57, 59

BIBLIOGRAPHY

Amundsen, Roald. *The North West Passage*. New York: E. P. Dutton, 1908.

Arima, Eugene. *Sketches of Anguhalluq. Inuktitut*, no. 62 (1985): 40–50. Ottawa: Indian and Northern Affairs.

Balikci, Asen. *The Netsilik Eskimo*. Garden City: Natural History Press, 1970.

Bellman, David (ed.). *Peter Pitseolak: Inuit Historian of Seekooseelak*. Montreal: McCord Museum, 1980.

Berenson, Bernard. *Seeing and Knowing*. London: Chapman and Hall, 1953.

Berton, Pierre. *The Arctic Grail*. New York: Viking Penguin, 1988.

Bilby, Julian W. *Among Unknown Eskimo*. London: Seeley Service, 1923.

Birket-Smith, Kaj. *Eskimos*. Copenhagen: Rhodos, 1971.

Blodgett, Jean. *Karoo Ashevak*. Winnipeg: Winnipeg Art Gallery, 1977.

— *The Coming and Going of the Shaman*. Winnipeg: Winnipeg Art Gallery, 1979.

— *Eskimo Narrative*. Winnipeg: Winnipeg Art Gallery, 1979.

— *Kenojuak*. Toronto: Firefly Books, 1985.

Blodgett, Jean, and Marie Bouchard. *Jessie Oonark: A Retrospective*. Winnipeg: Winnipeg Art Gallery, 1986.

Boas, Franz. *The Central Eskimo*. Sixth Annual Report of the Bureau of Ethnology, 399-669, Washington, 1888 (reprinted 1964).

— *Primitive Art*. New York: Dover Publications, 1955.

— *The Eskimo of Baffin Island and Hudson Bay*. New York: AMS Press, 1975.

Briggs, Jean L. *Never in Anger: Portrait of an Eskimo Family*. Cambridge, MA: Harvard University Press, 1970.

Brodzky, Anne T. (ed.). *Stone, Bones and Skin: Ritual and Shamanic Art*. Toronto: ArtsCanada, 1977.

Bruemmer, Fred. *Arctic Animals: A Celebration of Survival*. Toronto: McClelland and Stewart, 1986.

Buliard, Roger P. *Inuk*. London: Macmillan, 1963.

Butler, K. J., and Kay Bridge. *My Uncle Went to the Moon*. In Anne T. Brodzky (ed.), *Stone, Bones and Skin*, pp. 122-26. Toronto: ArtsCanada, 1977.

Carpenter, Edmund S. "Witch-Fear among the Aivilik Eskimos." *American Journal of Psychiatry*, vol. 110 (1953): 194-99.

— "The Timeless Present in the Mythology of the Aivilik Eskimos." *Anthropologica*, vol. 3 (1956): 1-4.

Clifford, James. *The Predicament of Culture*. Cambridge, MA: Harvard University Press, 1988.

Colombo, John Robert. *Poems of the Inuit*. Ottawa: Oberon Press, 1981.

Copland, A. Dudley. *Coplalook: Chief Trader, Hudson's Bay Company 1923–39*. Winnipeg: Watson and Dyer, 1985.

de Coccola, Raymond, and Paul King. *The Incredible Eskimo: Life among the Barren Land Eskimo*. Surrey, B.C.: Hancock House, 1987.

de Poncins, Gontran. *Kabloona*. New York: Reynal and Hitchcock, 1941.

Driscoll, Bernadette. *The Inuit Amautik*. Winnipeg: Winnipeg Art Gallery, 1980.

—*Inuit Myths, Legends and Songs*. Winnipeg: Winnipeg Art Gallery, 1982.

Eber, Dorothy H. *People from Our Side*. Edmonton: Hurtig Publishers, 1975.

—*Pitseolak: Pictures out of My Life*. Toronto: Oxford University Press, 1977.

— *When the Whalers Were Up North*. Montreal: McGill-Queen's University Press, 1989.

Elliott, George (ed.). *Sculpture Inuit*. Toronto: University of Toronto Press, 1971.

Flaherty, Robert. *Photographer/Filmmaker: The Inuit 1910-1922*. Vancouver: Vancouver Art Gallery, 1980.

Fleming, Archibald L. *Archibald the Arctic*. New York: Appleton-Century-Crofts, 1956.

Freuchen, Peter. *Eskimo*. New York: Horace Liveright, 1931.

—*Arctic Adventure*. New York: Farrar and Rinehart, 1935.

—*It's All Adventure*. New York: Farrar and Rinehart, 1938.

—*Vagrant Viking*. New York: Julian Messner, 1953.

—*Ice Floes and Flaming Water*. London: Travel Book Club, 1954.

—*I Sailed with Rasmussen*. New York: Julian Messner, 1958.

—*Book of the Eskimos*. Cleveland: World Publishing Company, 1961.

Freuchen, Peter, and Finn Salomensen. *The Arctic Year*. New York: G. P. Putnam's Sons, 1958.

Georgia. *Georgia: An Arctic Diary*. Edmonton: Hurtig Publishers, 1982.

Gilberg, Rolf. "Uisakavsak, 'The Big Liar.' " *Folk*, vol. 11-12 (1969/70): 83-95.

— "Changes in the Life of the Polar Eskimo." *Folk*, vol. 16-17 (1974/75): 159-70.

Graburn, Nelson. *Eskimos Without Igloos*. Boston: Little, Brown, 1969.

—*Eskimos of Northern Canada*, vols. 1, 2. New Haven: Human Relations Area Files, 1972.

Halifax, Joan. *Shaman: The Wounded Healer*. London: Thames and Hudson, 1982.

Hallendy, Norman E. *Reflections, Shades and Shadows*. Occasional Papers of the Prince of Wales Northern Heritage Centre, Yellowknife, Northwest Territories, 1985.

Harper, Kenn. *Give Me My Father's Body*. Frobisher Bay: Blacklead Books, 1986.

Hawkes, E. W. *The Labrador Eskimo*. Ottawa: Government Printing Bureau, 1916.

Henson, Matthew A. *A Negro Explorer at the North Pole*. New York: Arno Press, 1969.

Herbert, Wally. *The Noose of Laurels*. London: Hodder and Stoughton, 1989.

Hoffman, Walter J. *The Graphic Art of the Eskimos*. Smithsonian Institute Report, Washington, 1897.

Houston, James. *Eskimo Prints*. Barre, MA: Barre Publishers, 1971.

—*Songs of the Dream People*. Don Mills: Longman Canada, 1972.

Hunter, Archie. *Northern Traders: Caribou Hair in the Stew*. Victoria, B.C.: Sono Nis Press, 1983.

Iglauer, Edith. *The New People*. Garden City: Doubleday, 1966.

Jenness, Diamond. *The Life of the Copper Eskimos*. Report of the Canadian Arctic Expedition 1913-18, vol. 12, part A. New York: Johnson Reprint Corporation, 1970.

Lewis, Richard (ed.). *I Breathe a New Song*. New York: Simon and Schuster, 1971.

Lowenstein, Tom. *Eskimo Poems from Canada and Greenland*. Pittsburgh: University of Pittsburgh Press, 1973.

MacMillan, Donald B. *How Peary Reached the Pole*. New York: Houghton Mifflin, 1934.

Malaurie, Jean. *The Last Kings of Thule*. New York: E. P. Dutton, 1982.

Mamnguqsualuk, Victoria. *Keeveeok, Awake!* Edmonton: Boreal Institute for Northern Studies, University of Alberta, 1986.

Marsh, Donald B. *Echoes from a Frozen Land*. Edmonton: Hurtig Publishers, 1987.

Mathiassen, Therkel. *Archaeology of the Central Eskimos*. Report of the Fifth Thule Expedition, vol. 4, nos. 1, 2. Copenhagen, 1927.

—*Material Culture of the Iglulik Eskimos*. Report of the Fifth Thule Expedition, vol. 6, no. 1, Copenhagen, 1928.

Meldgaard, Jorgen. *Eskimo Sculpture*. New York: Clarkson N. Potter, 1960.

Millard, Peter. "Contemporary Inuit Art." *Arts Manitoba*, vol. 3, no. 1 (1983): 24-31.

Myers, Marybelle (ed.). *Davidialuk*. Montreal: La Fédération des Coopératives du Nouveau Québec, 1977.

—*Joe Talirunili*. Montreal: La Fédération des Coopératives du Nouveau Québec, 1977.

Nungak, Zebedee, and Eugene Arima. *Eskimo Stories: Unikkaatuat*. Ottawa: National Museums of Canada, Bulletin 235, 1969.

Oswalt, Wendell H. *Eskimos and Explorers*. Novato, CA: Chandler and Sharp, 1979.

Peary, Robert E. *The North Pole*. New York: Frederick A. Stokes, 1910.

Pryde, Duncan. *Nunaga: Ten Years of Eskimo Life*. New York: Walker, 1971.

Rasky, Frank. *The North Pole or Bust*. Toronto: McGraw-Hill Ryerson, 1977.

Rasmussen, Knud. *The People of the Polar North*. London: Kegan Paul, 1908.

—*Greenland by the Polar Sea*. London: Heinemann, 1921.

—*Eskimo Folk-Tales*. London, Copenhagen: Gyldendal, 1921.

—*Across Arctic America*. New York: G. P. Putnam's Sons, 1927.

—*Intellectual Culture of the Iglulik Eskimos*. Report of the Fifth Thule Expedition, vol. 7, no. 1. Copenhagen, 1929.

—*Intellectual Culture of the Caribou Eskimos*. Report of the Fifth Thule Expedition, vol. 7, no. 2. Copenhagen, 1930.

—*Iglulik and Caribou Eskimo Texts*. Report of the Fifth Thule Expedition, vol. 7, no. 3. Copenhagen, 1930.

—*The Netsilik Eskimos: Social Life and Spiritual Culture*. Report of the Fifth Thule Expedition, vol. 8, nos. 1, 2. Copenhagen, 1931.

—*Intellectual Culture of the Copper Eskimos*. Report of the Fifth Thule Expedition, vol. 9. Copenhagen, 1932.

—*Kagssagssuk: The Legend of the Orphan Boy*. Copenhagen: Lyngby Art Society, 1967.

Rink, Henrik. *Tales and Traditions of the Eskimo*. Montreal: McGill-Queen's University Press, 1974.

Roch, Ernst (ed.). *Arts of the Eskimo: Prints*. Montreal: Signum Press, 1974.

Ross, W. Gillies. *Whaling and Eskimos: Hudson Bay 1860-1915*. Ottawa: National Museum of Man, 1975.

Saladin d'Anglure, Bernard. *La Parole Changée en Pierre*. Quebec: Gouvernement du Québec, 1978.

Scherman, Katharine. *Spring on an Arctic Island*. Boston: Little, Brown, 1956.

Schwarz, Herbert T. *Elik: and Other Stories of the Mackenzie Eskimos*. Toronto: McClelland and Stewart, 1970.

Spencer, Robert F. *The North Alaskan Eskimo*. New York: Dover Publications, 1976.

Stefansson, Vilhjalmur. *My Life with the Eskimo*. New York: Macmillan, 1913.

Swinton, George. *Eskimo Sculpture*. Toronto: McClelland and Stewart, 1965.

—*Sculpture of the Eskimo*. Toronto: McClelland and Stewart, 1972.

Swinton, Nelda. *The Inuit Sea Goddess*. Montreal: Musée des Beaux-Arts, 1980.

Tagoona, Armand. *Shadows*. Toronto: Oberon Press, 1975.

Thomson, George Malcolm. *The Search for the North-West Passage*. New York: Macmillan, 1975.

Turner, Lucien M. *Indians and Eskimos in the Quebec-Labrador Peninsula*. Quebec: Presses Comeditex, 1979.

Valentine, Victor F., and Frank G. Vallee. *Eskimo of the Canadian Arctic*. Toronto: McClelland and Stewart, 1968.

Vallee, Frank G. *Kabloona and Eskimo in the Central Keewatin*. Ottawa: Department of Northern Affairs, 1962.

van den Steenhoven, Geert. *Leadership and Law Among the Eskimos of the Keewatin District*. Leiden: Leiden University, 1962.

Weyer, Edward M. *The Eskimos: Their Environment and Folkways*. New Haven: Yale University Press, 1932.

Wilkinson, Doug. *Land of the Long Day*. Toronto: McClelland and Stewart, 1968.

Williams, Stephen G. *In the Middle: The Eskimo Today*. Boston: Godine, 1983.

Williamson, Robert G. *Eskimo Underground: Socio-Cultural Change in the Canadian Central Arctic*. Uppsala: Uppsala University, 1974.

Zaslow, Morris. *The Northward Expansion of Canada 1914-1967*. Toronto: McClelland and Stewart, 1988.

Zepp, Norman. *Pure Vision: The Keewatin Spirit*. Regina: University of Regina, 1986.

INDEX OF ARTISTS

INDEX